The Worst of Cricket

Nigel Henderson

Run outs to riots: Malice and misfortune in the world's cruellest game

2

The Worst of Cricket

Nigel Henderson

Run outs to riots:
Malice and misfortune in
the world's cruellest game

The Worst of Cricket

Run outs to riots: Malice and misfortune in the world's cruellest game

© Nigel Henderson

Nigel Henderson has asserted his rights in accordance with the Copyright, Designs and Patents Act 1988 to be identified as the author of this work.

Publishing by:

Pitch Publishing (Brighton) Ltd
10 Beresford Court
Somerhill Road
Hove BN3 1RH
Email: info@pitchpublishing.co.uk
Web: www.pitchpublishing.co.uk

First published 2004.

ISBN 0-9542460-4-7

Picture credits:

Empics: Pages; 11, 45, 197, 221, 247.

Hulton Archive/Getty Images:
Pages; 27, 95, 123, 145, 169.

Reuters: Page 71.

Editor: Roy Chuter

Cover and page design:

Luke Jefford & Associates
3 St. George's Place
Brighton
East Sussex
BN1 4GA
Tel: 01273 600639

Printed and bound in Great Britain by The Cromwell Press

Contents

Foreword by Mark Steel

When I was about thirteen, as part of my chosen obsession I decided I would read every single cricket book owned by Swanley library. It wasn't until I was about halfway through the twentieth book that it dawned on me almost every one of these books had been excruciatingly boring. I'd read endless accounts of how many runs Patsy Hendren or Jack Hobbs had scored on this or that day, but that, to anyone who wasn't there, is as meaningless as reading a list of winning lottery numbers – or losing ones, come to that.

The tedious statistics would be interspersed with gushing prose of old players. I seem to remember passages such as, "It is said that when Sandham played his famous cover drive, passing milk-maids would swoon and collapse into the Brighton Road." And they all seemed to mention a poem that would apparently have been written at the time, something like, "O to be in Gloucester / When Grace goes out to bat / 114 not out followed by 5 for 63 / My goodness, fancy that."

The tone and language of the vast volume of cricket literature contained little that could connect to a 1970s boy at a Kent comprehensive. Nor was it a sentiment that flowed only from old books. Within the world of radio commentary, there seemed to be a rule that decreed that, whenever play was interrupted by rain, the time would be filled with an incomprehensible interview with someone called Sir Percy or the Duke of Pembroke.

They would recall, in an accent I'd only ever heard on Monty Python, a certain umpire on the Ashes tour of 1893, who would end each day's play by saying, "Gentlemen, I hereby assert that proceedings are adjourned," and everyone would fall about laughing. At times it felt as if at any moment an official would burst into your living room and demand to know why you were watching without wearing a tie. It was as if the exhilaration, grace and joy I derived from the game was diametrically opposite to the pompous manner in which it was officially recorded.

For example, I was lucky enough to have stood amidst the carnival that bustled, thumped and bugled around the Oval as Viv Richards swiped 291 off a despairing England attack. The innings, and the exuberance with which it was received, were a celebration of the human spirit, and their story couldn't be told in the colonial house style that dominated English cricket writing. Nor could that style have described the atmosphere that crackled from the other side of the world the previous year, when Dennis Lillee and Jeff Thomson exploded with an aggression that appalled much of the English cricket establishment.

From around that time, there seems to have arisen a new generation of cricket enthusiasts, resulting in a clash of cultures as wide as the time when the punk movement polarised the generations throughout the rest of society. For the next few years, it seemed that anyone who popularised the game would fall foul of the authorities. Ian Botham was cast as a perennial rebel. So, to a slightly lesser extent, was David Gower, to the point that one day after a heroic 70 against the foreboding West Indies pace attack, he was officially reprimanded for batting in blue socks.

To society as a whole, Botham and Gower appear as fairly conservative figures, but to those who ran English cricket they were Joe Strummer and Sid Vicious. Worst of all, the flamboyance of the crowds was seen as a threat that had to be stamped out. Music was banned, flags were banned, the standing areas were closed, and the famous arena of debauchery in front of the Lord's Tavern bar was built over. The result is the impressive achievement of holding Test matches involving the West Indies and Asian nations, which hardly anyone from the West Indies or Asian nations wants to go and watch.

But, bit by bit, the new generation is breaking through. Television coverage now attempts to explain the game to the newcomer without being patronising. And most cricket reporters now appear to be people who have heard of Eminem, or at least Jimi Hendrix. Most notably, several books about cricket seem to be written by authors who inhabit the same world as the rest of the population, except they have a peculiar obsession with this peculiar game.

That sense is one of the joys of this volume. It's a book that celebrates the quirkiness of cricket, and the author has brought together a splendid collection of the quirkiest bits of all. The old style of writing would insist the umpire's decision was saintly. This book gives us accounts of the worst umpiring decisions ever. The old style would tut in shame at the merest departure from due reverence on the field. This book has a chapter called "The Worst Tantrums."

But while it revels in these oddities, it's every bit as much about cricket as any academic approach to the subject, for it understands that the drama that drives sport is not the technicalities but the sub-plots. Millions cheered when Muhammad Ali knocked out George Foreman, because they saw it as a triumph of principles, defiance and flamboyance. Every jangle of tin cans and hooting of klaxons that greeted those runs of Viv Richards that day, was charged with the sub-plot that, before

the series, the white South African who captained England had said, "We will make the West Indies grovel."

This is a book for anyone who cherishes the sub-plots, the human aspects, the soap opera that makes sport so absorbing. It's a book for anyone who can identify with the sense of awe I felt on April 12th 2004, as I sat outside a Little Chef, desperately adjusting a radio for the best reception. And I listened as Brian Lara, a man who astounded the world ten years earlier by breaking a seemingly impregnable record, but subsequently hit a series of social problems, and had recently been pilloried throughout the Caribbean as captain of a failing team, broke the record all over again. It may not be a book for those who can identify with my partner, who watched me in amazement and said, "You weren't this emotional when our children were born."

Introduction

We've been swallowing the myth for years – propagated by upstanding public school headmasters, officer material, and men in garish yellow and orange ties – that cricket is a gentlemanly pursuit, where bad luck is something to be borne stoically and bad behaviour poor form that will get us drummed out of the club.

This is plainly nonsense.

The only element that stands up to closer scrutiny is that cricket is the game of life: not the life where we all learn by our mistakes, shrug off our failures and live to fight another day, but the life that's the bitch who gives us a hard time before we die.

This book is a warts and all celebration of that truth: that cricket is sometimes so bad to us, that we have no option than to be complete bastards back to it, irrespective of the image of the game or the effect it will have on youngsters (not to mention sponsors).

It'll make you realise that cricket is, and always has been, a wolf in sheep's clothing (though heavily-dyed for one-dayers under lights), a game that despite its constant attempts to walk a straight line, regularly veers off into full nervous breakdown.

So sit forward and shake your fists at the temerity of the worst cricket tantrums, sit back and shake your head at the worst cricket riots, and sit down to stop your knees knocking at the sight of the worst cricket injuries, among other subjects – all from the first-class game.

Chapter One

The worst
umpiring
decisions

The Worst Umpiring Decisions

English umpire Don Oslear was once so upset when he realised he'd erroneously fingered Viv Richards in a Test that he sought out the West Indies skipper afterwards and apologised. It's hard to imagine the two officials who took charge of one match on the MCC's tour to India in 1952 doing the same. Like those Mafia godfathers who administer lavish affection on their own yet swear a rather grisly vengeance on anyone who threatens their 'family', the pair, whom for the reason that history does not relate their names, we shall call A. Non and Y. Mous, would jump for joy when giving out an English batsman but dissolve into tears when forced to decide against their own side.

Suspicions of bias, incompetence and plain bad eyesight are inexorably tied up with cricket officialdom over the ages but rarely has the cricketing fraternity been prepared to face, head on, a much more insidious cause of rotten umpiring: sadism, pure and simple. Few officials in any sport are truly rounded individuals and the frustrations of standing still all day while people in the prime of life periodically yell at you can have a damaging effect on the psyche. So here, restoring that element to its rightful place in the pantheon of questionable umpiring decisions, are the 12 worst examples of the art, perhaps ever…

1 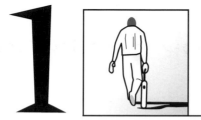 A.E. Street (England)
Somerset v Sussex
County Championship. Taunton. May 1919.

An extraordinary decision to end an extraordinary match, Mr Street wins his place in umpiring history as the only man in first-class cricket to uphold an appeal for "timed out". The unfortunate victim of this incredible stickler for the rules was Harold John Heygate. Stricken with rheumatism, the stylish Sussex opener (so stylish he only played six games between 1903 and 1919) nevertheless was forced to bat at No 11 with the scores tied. His extended crawl to the wicket was agonising to witness, but worse was to follow as he finally winched himself up to some semblance of a stance. A Somerset fielder with a sadistic nature suggested he had taken longer than the legal two minutes, Mr Street agreed and hastily removed the stumps and marched off.

White Stick Rating
1/10

Some reports suggest the humiliated Heygate never played again and died several years later a lonely, gnarled and bitter man, others that he's still making his way back to the pavilion.

2

C.S. Elliott & J.H. Parks (England)

Northamptonshire v Gloucestershire

County Championship. Peterborough. May 1961.

Gloucestershire captain **Charles Pugh suffered an appalling injury in this match** when a delivery from John Larter broke his jaw in two places. Had he been able to move his mouth he might have responded with a well-chosen expletive when he realised he'd also been given out lbw. For nought. The records fail to inform us which of these hard-hearted officials administered the fateful decision but it must be assumed he wasn't the most welcome of visitors to Pugh's hospital bedside.

White Stick Rating

8/10

Well, maybe he didn't get his chin outside the line of off stump; perhaps he did play no shot...

3

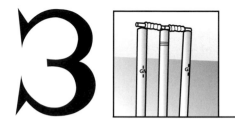

Lou Rowan (Australia)
Australia v England
1st Test. Brisbane. Nov/Dec 1970.

This former policeman, who later on this tour had serious run-ins with England fast bowler John Snow, first incurred the tourists' wrath in the opening Test at the Gabba. Keith Stackpole, one of a long line of stocky Australian batsmen, pushed a ball towards Boycott in the covers for a seemingly safe single, only to see the lop-grinned Yorkshireman throw down the stumps at the bowler's end as he struggled manfully to make up the ground. Although Rowan ruled for the batsman, a sharp-shuttered local photographer captured the bat a foot short and the image was splashed around the Aussie papers by the evening.

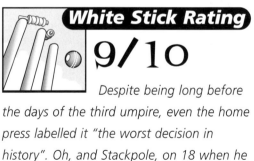

White Stick Rating
9/10

Despite being long before the days of the third umpire, even the home press labelled it "the worst decision in history". Oh, and Stackpole, on 18 when he received his reprieve, went on to score 207.

15

4 Shakeel Khan (Pakistan)
Pakistan v England
1st Test. Lahore. November 1987.

England's tour of the sub-continent provided a vintage selection for connoisseurs of umpiring decisions bizarre, biased and just plain bad. Everyone remembers Shakoor Rana's contribution to the contretemps with Mike Gatting in the second Test at Faisalabad (of which, more later) but that somewhat overshadowed the exploits of Shakeel at Lahore. The 36-year-old bank employee was calculated to be responsible for seven out of nine dubious decisions against England, who slid to a four-day innings defeat. Abdul Oadir benefited from Shakeel's benevolence to the tune of record figures of 9-56 but in a strange outworking of karma, received the worst decision of the game himself when he was given out stumped before Bruce French had removed the bails.

White Stick Rating

11/10

Shakeel lifted awful umpiring to a whole new plane, giving lbws that were not only missing leg stump, but missing another leg stump as well. It was noted by one observer that he gave his rulings with such incautious speed they had no chance of going through his brain first.

5

David Constant (England)
England v Pakistan
3rd Test. Headingley. August 1982.

Constant. The name suggests something unshakeable and unwavering, stability, reliability, even affability. To some touring sides, however, he was simply a liability, and some believe that a Constant decision in this series decider was the catalyst for England-Pakistan ill-feeling. The match had reached a critical stage on the third evening when the wiry tail-ender Sikander Bakht, who had added a crucial 30 with Imran Khan in 70 minutes, pushed forward and the ball lobbed up to short leg. England's close fielders exploded with a beautifully-rehearsed appeal, despite replays showing the ball had missed the bat by the width of Kirkstall Lane. But

Constant held up his forefinger, and Sikander's humiliation was complete when he realised the bowler was Vic Marks.

White Stick Rating

6/10

Imran demanded neutral umpires in international games and Pakistan objected to Constant standing on their next tour in 1987 – a request given short shrift by the TCCB. Thus followed Shakeel, Shakoor Rana, a contretemps oversweaters, and accusations of ball-tampering, before Mike Atherton and Wasim Akram took the sting out of hostilities.

6

Har Sharma (India)
North Zone v Australia
Tour match. Jullunder. November 1969.

Indian batsmen are supposedly renowned for their expertise in dealing with spin bowling, but they had never come across anyone like John Gleeson before. The Australian had mastered a technique in which he bent his middle finger behind the ball enabling him to bowl leg-breaks with an off-break action. So bewildered were the North Zone players as Gleeson racked up a 17–over spell in their first innings that they struggled to lay a bat on the ball, prodding, groping and plopping forward but finding only thin air or, when they did make contact, escaping, thanks to the fumbling fingers of the Aussie fielders or the utter incompetence of the umpires.

It was some relief for the visitors, then, when Vinay Lamba, the North Zone opener, finally obliged by getting the clearest of edges that wicketkeeper Brian Taber at last held on to. The whole team appealed with one voice, but Har Sharma, as before, remained motionless. Surprised but undaunted, players from as far away as the covers and mid-off advanced closer to the umpire and put the question, perhaps not as politely, a second time. This time, Sharma's finger shot up, and he followed the apparent change of mind with the explanation that there was such a strong wind blowing, it had taken some time for the noise of the snick to reach his end.

White Stick Rating

7/10

Hearing aid as well for Mr Sharma.

19

7

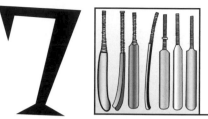

Douglas Sang-Hue
(West Indies)
West Indies v Pakistan
2nd Test. Trinidad. March 1977

Years before Mike Atherton managed to run himself out on 99 at Lord's (see chapter 9). West Indies opener Roy Fredericks did the same at Trinidad. Only he didn't. Well, not according to Mr Sang Hue, who turned down a confident appeal and went on to preside over a comfortable win for the home side (Fredericks 120). He later told Pakistan skipper Mushtaq Mohammad that Fredericks had been out but "you don't have to live here".

White Stick Rating
5/10

All this is alleged in an Imran Khan autobiography, so it must be true. After all, as Ian Botham and Alan Lamb know, Imran would be the last person to get involved in any form of litigation.

8

A.R. Joshi (India)
India v West Indies
5th Test. Bombay. February 1949.

Darrell Hair, the Australian umpire much admired by Muttiah Muralitharan for his microscopic attention to detail when it comes to the degree of curvature of the bowling arm, made a late play for inclusion here when he marched off England, three wickets from defeating the Old Enemy, a minute early on the final day of the third Test of the 1994/95 Ashes series in Sydney only to have to resume for four balls when Mike Atherton pointed out the necessity of an accurate wristwatch. But AR Joshi was in a league of his own when it came to premature ejaculations: when he called "time" on India's 1948/49 series against the West Indies in Bombay, the home side, who had needed 361 in even time to square the rubber, required just six more runs to win. Not only had Joshi allowed just five balls in the penultimate over, his action of removing the bails served to prevent a final over when there were still 90 seconds left on the clock to complete the match.

White Stick Rating

10/10

For its sheer historical impact, Joshi's error deserves recognition. Victory would have been his nation's first over the West Indies. In the event, India had to wait another 23 years to record that achievement.

9

Atio Khan (Pakistan)
Pakistan v South Africa
One day International. Lahore. October 1994.

Ah yes, the wonders of technology. These would put an end to the fallibility of the two men on the field. However, even the third umpire cannot legislate for mistakes by the... third umpire. Dave Richardson, the South Africa wicketkeeper, had stretched to make his ground while taking a quick single in this Wills Series one-dayer and while he had appeared to the naked eye to have made it, the decision was referred to the Pakistani official seated in front of his television monitor to confirm the judgement. Mr Khan's task seemed clear enough. He concurred with his colleague's decision and, his hand poised above two coloured buttons, he prepared to reprieve the batsman by opting for green. Unfortunately for Richardson, and to the delight of the home crowd, something got lost in translation and the light that shone resonantly from the scoreboard was of a more crimson hue.

White Stick Rating
2/10

Mr Khan may not have been in desperate need of a guide dog, but the Pakistan board had to answer some awkward questions when it was discovered he was colour-blind. Needless to say, he has since been removed from his day job in an Islamabad nuclear bunker.

10

B.C. Cooray (Sri Lanka)
Sri Lanka v England
2nd Test. Kandy. February 2001.

In another match famous for a plethora of umpiring mistakes – 15 at the last count – the Sri Lankan unleashed the worst on the home team captain Sanath Jayasuriya, creating an explosive atmosphere on a day that had been designated one of peace by the local Buddhists. Caddick bounded in from the jauntily named Buddhist Research Institute End to bowl his first delivery of the second innings to Jayasuriya, who flayed at a widish ball and was miraculously caught by a horizontal Graham Thorpe at third slip. The catch was so good that Cooray could not bear to give it not out despite the fact that Jayasuriya had clearly banged the ball into the ground first. The next thing to hit the ground was, surprisingly, not BC himself, but Jayasuriya's helmet, hurled in anger by the opener as he trudged incredulously to the pavilion.

White Stick Rating
9/10

Cooray, also famed for fingering Nasser Hussain lbw when he had edged a ball for four, was accused by the local media of batting for England as the touring team went on to square the three-match series.

23

11

David Shepherd (England)
England v Pakistan
2nd Test. Old Trafford. May/June 2001.

Technology, of course, has the ability to make idiots of us all. Witness your most recent holiday video, for example. But when it exposes the deficiencies of a national treasure, it is enough to create widespread study of the navel. Had the second Test between England and Pakistan petered out to an insignificant draw, Shep, as he is affectionately known, would have retained his position as close to the hearts of the people as his namesake pet dog on Blue Peter. Unfortunately, Shep's focus on bat, pad, glove and other parts of product and person made him neglect Saqlain Mushtaq's constant over-stepping of the crease. As four of the eight England wickets that fell for 60 runs late on the final afternoon, condemning them to an unlikely defeat, were revealed to be no-balls, so notions of our premier umpire's infallibility were shockingly dispelled.

White Stick Rating

2/10

It's been suggested that

TV replays, in close-up and super slo-mo and with the help of Hawk-eye, merely emphasise how many decisions umpires actually get right. This is not so. They unequivocally show how many umpires get wrong – loads. So let's not be too harsh on Shep, who took his eye off the ball for a couple of hours and was haunted enough by these recurring images to have to be talked out of resignation by the ECB.

12

Twelfth Man
Frank Chester

One of the finest umpires of his generation, Chester became embittered later on not only because his loss of an arm in the First World War encouraged batsmen to try and hit sixes when he was standing at their end. That injury had halted a promising playing career and Chester had to be content with an officiating role in the game, where he indulged his love for the horses by offering tips to fielders standing at square leg. He also stood in Australia, but by 1946, as England were overwhelmed by the Antipodeans, he became less enamoured of his cousins from Down Under, publicly criticising their over-zealous appealing. Seven years later he was removed from duty, the MCC citing illness, after a number of contentious decisions and complaints from the touring team that he had started turning down appeals in a mock Australian accent.

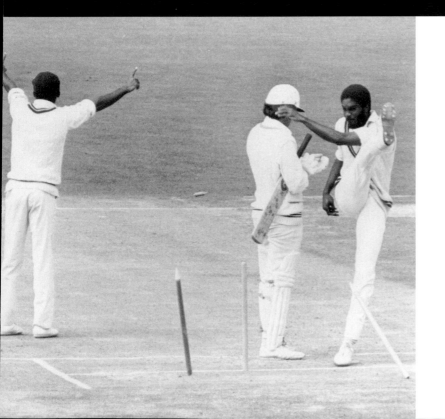

Chapter Two

The Worst
Tantrums

The Worst Tantrums

The powers that be may splutter into their Darjeeling and mumble behind their monocles and handlebar moustaches, but the fact of the matter is that umpires, for all their protestations that they're doing their best, haven't got the benefit of slow-motion replays. How would you like to stand out there for seven hours a day etc. etc. having to bear their share of the responsibility for the ugliest displays of player misbehaviour? It seems appropriate, therefore, that this category should follow directly in their footsteps. Of course, cricketing bureaucrats have their role too, along with crowds and the players' own dubious temperaments, as we shall see...

1

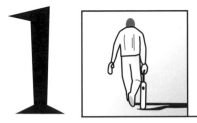

David Boon
Australia v New Zealand
One-day international. Brisbane. January 1988.

Outwardly undemonstrative, it was once said of the stocky Tasmanian, who became one of Australia's leading run scorers, that he had "ice in his veins". Mainly Foster's Ice. Part barman and part bushman, nothing would faze him, whether it was sinking a record 53 cans of XXXX on the Qantas 747 from Sydney to London, or sucking the equally toxic venom of a black mamba from an injured ranch hand's calf muscle (in fact, any reptile unlucky enough to be caught by his intimidating stare would have probably removed its own poison). Actually, there was one thing that would make the one-time Durham skipper pause for thought. His mum. Adjudged leg-before to Martin Snedden in Brisbane, he fired off a volley of swear words in the direction of umpire Mel Johnson as he stomped back towards the pavilion and subsequently escaped with an official reprimand only after she rang the dressing-room and ordered him not to react like that again.

On the Richter scale

Just 3.5 for the silent assassin who turned out to be a mummy's boy.

2

Colin Croft
and Michael Holding
West Indies v New Zealand
1st & 2nd Tests. Dunedin & Christchurch. Feb 1980

If Michael Holding's flowing but lethal bowling style was known as Whispering Death, Colin Croft was Murder and Mayhem whose arrival was announced by megaphone. When Croft wasn't rattling the skeletons of the home batsmen, he was shaking the sensibilities of the Kiwi supporters by suggesting that if he was ever shipwrecked off the New Zealand coast he'd turn round and swim past the sharks to Australia. He wasn't a great advocate of their umpires either and when one, Fred Goodall, consistently no-balled him at Christchurch, he veered away from his run up sufficiently to barge the poor official over. Later, the whole West Indies team refused to come out after tea unless Goodall was removed, and the manager of the side, Willie

Rodriguez, insinuated there was a conspiracy between the New Zealand administration and its umpires to ensure a home victory. Goodall was not replaced and at the resumption a number of West Indies players displayed their displeasure by instituting a work-to-rule, refusing to field balls propelled in their direction and allowing Geoff Howarth to complete his century in the process. Relations had first soured in Dunedin when Holding was on the raw end of some controversial officiating: when one particularly confident appeal went unanswered, the usually placid paceman raced up to the batsman's stumps and uprooted the leg and the off (no easy accomplishment) with one swing of his size 13 boot.

On the Richter scale

A meagre 2.5 for Croft, who wins few marks for subtlety, but a whopping 7.9 for Holding, who found that style didn't desert him even in a rage. Just observe that follow through – the way the Jamaican's toe finishes level with his forehead.

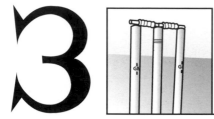

3

Abdul Qadir
West Indies v Pakistan
3rd Test. Bridgetown. April 1988.

The Royal Barbados Police got their priorities right when Qadir leapt over the boundary fence and landed a punch on 21-year-old car wash attendant Albert August: they waited until the West Indies had secured a two-wicket win before marching the Pakistani leg spinner down to the local nick on an assault charge. The problems started when that old chestnut, an lbw appeal, was turned down. Qadir and his team-mates swarmed round umpire David Archer pleading with him to uphold the demand. It took Imran Khan, the captain, some moments to restore order before Qadir snatched his cap from Archer and stormed off to long leg, where he was roundly jeered and taunted by the home spectators. Still fizzing like one of his more effective googlies, he became embroiled in a heated exchange of opinions with about 20 people close to the boundary rope. It wasn't long before the discourse turned distasteful and the Pakistan management was having to pay $500 in compensation to keep Qadir out of court.

On the Richter scale

6.5 raised to 8 on appeal when it was realised that Qadir had been in sufficient control of his faculties to use his left fist, thus ensuring his spinning fingers were not exposed to danger.

32

4

Dennis Lillee
Australia v England
1st Test. Perth. December 1979.

Cricket is recognisable by its sounds as well as its sights. The steady murmur of a first morning Test crowd, the sudden, sometimes blood-curdling cries of 'howzat???', and the consoling knock of leather on aluminium. Aluminium? Yes, this was the match in which Lillee literally showed his metal, coming out to take on England's bowlers with a bat made of the stuff. However, England captain Mike Brearley displayed some mettle of his own, stubbornly complaining to the umpires about its impact on the ball. When Lillee was told to exchange it for a bat sculpted from more orthodox materials, he became a very angry young Dennis, storming about trying to make his moustache look fierce before hurling his bat towards extra cover and being brought a replacement.

On the Richter scale

A reverberating 9.3. Not content simply to marry arrogance and abusiveness, Lillee threw in a slice of equipment violation for good measure. Top tantrum.

5

Sunil Gavaskar
Australia v India
3rd Test. Melbourne. February 1981.

Walk-offs are rare in cricket, but even more rarely effective. They are the spoilsport action of the boy in the playground who owns all the equipment and disappears with it in a fit of pique when he's out. On this occasion at the MCG, the boy also tried to persuade his best mate to go with him: the Indian opener, disgusted with his lbw decision after a decent score of 70 had almost doubled his tour aggregate, hauled his bemused partner Chetan Chauhan as far as the pavilion gate before the team manager, Squadron Leader Shahid Durrani, of the Indian Air Force, clipped their wings. The pair were then told, in no uncertain terms, that any more nonsense would see them returned to the hotel without any tea.

On the Richter scale

5.6 An earthquake which would have sent after-shocks circumnavigating the cricket world was only averted by Mr Durrani's early response system. While the Australians stood around contemplating a couple of days off courtesy of an Indian forfeiture, Dilip Vengsarkar was sent for to accompany Chauhan back to the middle.

6

John Snow and Ray Illingworth
Australia v England
Sixth/Seventh Test. Sydney. February 1971.

To watch Snow, England's premier fast bowler of the late Sixties and early Seventies, in action was akin to observing poetry in motion. But the Sussex paceman, deadly from 22 yards, showed an equal appreciation of metre and rhythm off the pitch, publishing two volumes of his own verse. If he liked to read as well as write, he probably found some satisfaction in the compositions of future poet laureate Ted Hughes and his dispassionate observations on the brutality of the natural world. Snow had a similarly detached approach to the perils of facing rapid, short-pitched bowling and was none too pleased when, having sent Terry Jenner back to the pavilion bleeding profusely from a head wound incurred from a bouncer, he was cautioned by umpire Lou Rowan for intimidation. Rowan's warning was met, the umpire claimed, not by mature acceptance from Snow and his captain, Illingworth, but by a short, succinct barrage of words which definitely failed to scan. When an incensed crowd began to throw beer cans at Snow at the end of the over, Illy ordered his team from the field.

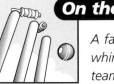

On the Richter scale

A faltering 4.5. The whining couplet, and their team-mates, were forced to resume play when told that if they didn't Australia would be awarded the match.

7

Chris Broad

Pakistan v England 1st Test. Lahore. November 1987.

Australia v England

Only Test. Sydney. January/February 1988.

By rights, Chris Broad should have been born an Aussie. Almost everything about him, from his upright stance at the crease – with a not inconsiderable backside thrust towards square leg – to his tortoise-like progress to the pavilion after being given out, screamed Attitude with a capital A. That, though, would have been to ignore some purely English traits that enabled the selectors to append that description with a couple of capital Ps – for Problem, yes, but mainly Petulance. The Bristol-born Gloucestershire and Nottinghamshire left-hander might have got away with such behaviour at home, but his major crimes were committed on foreign fields, specifically those of Pakistan and Down Under.

Becoming one of Shakeel Khan's "victims" at Lahore (see chapter one), he declined to accept the umpire's ruling, gesturing defiantly that he hadn't edged Qasim to the wicket-keeper. Only the consoling arm of Graham Gooch, his opening partner, eventually persuaded him to leave the arena. Then, not content with a hard-fought 139 in the Bicentennial Test at the SCG, his response to a slightly unfortunate dismissal was to turn round and flat bat the middle stump into the northern hemisphere. The trademark reluctance of his return to the dressing-room was played out to a chorus of Aussie boos.

On the Richter scale

8.8. The England selectors, invoking a capital L, had the last laugh. When a double failure at Lord's followed in the second home Test of the summer against the West Indies, his international career lay in ruins. Although he emerged from the debris to post continually impressive county performances, a crumbling hip-joint forced his retirement, naturally an unwilling one, in 1993.

8

Graham Dilley
New Zealand v England
1st Test. Christchurch. February 1988.

One swear word is understandable, two forgivable if exploring the boundaries, but a trio of expletives, clearly intoned in finest Estuary English as if specifically for the consumption of the spectators in the back row of the Mound Stand, can be expensive. So it transpired for the one-time Kent quickie, whose recent upheaval in leaving Canterbury – in a show of solidarity when opening batsman and brother-in-law Graham Johnson was sacked – had no doubt combined with a long and trying winter to send him over the edge. In a classic case of a straw breaking the camel's back, Dilley, despite recording a Test-career best of six for 38, got the hump when the third of three consecutive confident appeals, a bat-pad claim against Martin Crowe, went unrewarded. Subsequent dallying over whether to take his sweater from umpire Brian Aldridge before marching off without it failed to endear him to the Kiwi crowd or his own team management, who fined him $250.

On the Richter scale

7.1. It ain't what you do, it's the way that you do it: Dilley's ear-splitting expression of the anatomically-unattainable wins in the style stakes what it loses in content and originality.

9

Sylvester Clarke
Pakistan v West Indies
4th Test. Multan. December/January 1980/81.

A gentle giant off the field, Clarke, the only Test cricketer known to possess the middle name Theophilus, would disguise his short-pitched armoury in an ambling run-up which he utilised to lull the batsman into a false sense of security before unleashing a delivery which would generally shock, most definitely awe and soon have him reaching for the white flag. But like many a bowling bully, he was more readily able to give than receive, and when the Pakistan supporters started pelting him with their own weapons of crass destruction – orange peel and pistachio nuts – he responded like a bear with a sore head and inflicted the same upon a student leader whose skull took a glancing blow from the boundary block he picked up and launched into the crowd.

On the Richter scale

9.8. Clarke's retaliation sparked a mini-riot as the student leader was carted off to hospital, dazed and bruised, and necessitated his skipper, Alvin Kallicharran, going down on bended knee in front of the enraged Ibn-e-Qasim Bagh Stadium crowd to act as a calming influence.

10

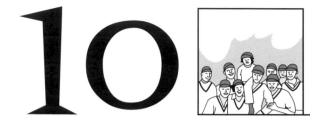

William Barnes
Australia v England
3rd Test. Sydney. February 1885.

The presence of a prefix was almost a prerequisite in top-class English cricket in the late 19th century. But to be found among a predominance of Lords, the occasional Colonel, a smattering of Drs and a rare Sir was an all-rounder of common Nottinghamshire stock whose only moniker, should he have been afforded one, would have been Right Dishonourable. Billy Barnes's list of ignominious actions included once missing several matches on a tour to Australia after he injured his hand in a ruck with an opposing captain; he perhaps only retained his place with his titled team-mates because he truly had no peer when it came to hitting hundreds or weeding out critical wickets while roaring drunk. Well, that's when he could be persuaded to pad up or turn his medium-paced arm over. Arthur Shrewsbury, the England captain, was to feel the bitter end of Barnes's notorious distaste for authority only days after asserting confidently that the player's "visits to the land of the Golden Fleece" – lager to you and me – were a thing of the past. They weren't. And when he turned to the potential match-winner to ease them out of a sticky situation in the field at the SCG, Barnes took out his passive-aggression by simply refusing to bowl. In either innings.

On the Richter scale

3.7 Barnes eventually found the life he was born to, taking over as landlord of the Angel Inn.

41

11

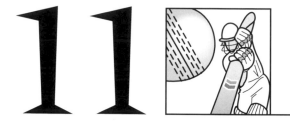

Javed Miandad
Pakistan v England
(World Cup group match.
Rawalpindi. October 1987)

Mohammed Javed Miandad Khan is a bit of a mouthful for any commentator, not to mention a logistical nightmare for scorecard printers, so it is no surprise that the man who was to become a legend of Pakistan cricket decided early in his career he wanted to be known solely by his two middle names. While Miandad became his widely-used sobriquet, evoking images of a young boy and his old man playing a dustbins-for-wickets form of the game in the back streets of Karachi, it remains of uncertain origin. Javed, on the other hand, has its roots in the linguistics of ancient Persia and means, literally, "eternally", fitting enough for a mercurial middle-order master who has had a myriad of reincarnations as player, captain and coach of his national side, and who has been a recurring pain in the posterior for many an opponent. Chief among them might be Mike Gatting, whose no doubt eloquent attempts to hurry Miandad back to the pavilion in Rawalpindi – the batsman was rooted to the spot after being given out lbw, not something he was used to in his home country – were like a red rag to a bull. The simmering Miandad boiled over, spinning round to smack Gatting firmly across his chubby chops before flouncing off the field.

On the Richter scale

4.2 Miandad later claimed that Gatting had sworn at him, an accusation denied by the Middlesex man. Whoever's nearer the truth, it hardly merited the Pakistani accompanying his blow with a threat to do the squat Englishman terminal harm.

12  Twelfth Man

We all have different reactions to the ordeal of defeat: some of us find solace by locating a scapegoat and handily displacing our disappointment on to them, while others of us simply make for the nearest pub to immerse our sorrows in drink. In Islamabad, the former, in the shape of stringing up a dummy of the offending character to the nearest tree and subjecting it to countless indignities, retains some popularity but is considered by others to be old hat, while the latter, in this city of the alcohol-free, is not really an option. Not that the alternative response one resident had to the elimination of his country in the quarter-final of the 1996 World Cup is necessarily to be recommended. Picking up his trusty AK-47, he took aim at the scenes of Sri Lankan jubilation on his television screen and blasted them from his field of vision. No doubt, as he cooled down, he would have realised that this was no meagre crime: televisions were in short supply in the city, citizens having to make do with one set between ten. Determined not to lose face further, he did just that, in fact, by turning the gun on himself and pulling the trigger. A terminal tantrum if ever there was one.

Chapter Three

The Worst Confrontations

The Worst Confrontations

Mike Brearley once observed that cricket is unique among team games in that its major confrontations are between individuals; Dr Brearley did not become an esteemed analyst of the human condition without good reason. Mostly these confrontations are overwhelmingly positive, not only defining the nature of a sporting contest but also creating the conditions in which one principal player allows the other at least a moment in the spotlight, if not quite equal billing. Sir Garry Sobers, for example, was a batsman so secure at centre stage that he could afford to acknowledge the bowler's own skill in making him adjust to a late swinging delivery – before smacking the ball through mid-wicket for four. Sadly, as we shall see, there is a sizeable – some might say increasing – number of instances which do not measure up to such fine ideals. Disclaimer: the over-representation of Australians in this section is purely intentional.

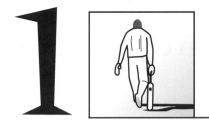

Merv Hughes v Mark Greatbatch

New Zealand v Australia

3rd Test. Auckland. March 1993.

Electrolysis may be the byword of the Bondi beach bum these days – but, in the past, many an Aussie was defined by his facial hair. Bristling with aggression as well as a rather impressive moustache, the prime example of this species was Merv Hughes – a man descended directly from the walrus. Not content with drawing attention to himself in this way, the Victorian had a whirling bowling action which created such momentum that he was usually unable to bring himself to a halt before he was within a couple of steps of the batsman, eyeball to eyeball, spitting in the direction of his opponent's size 12s and preparing to select a few well-worn phrases from his encyclopaedia of expletives. It was an intimidating sight for any opener stuck submissively in his crease –

even for one of equivalent bulk in Mark Greatbatch, the New Zealand left-hander. After a tense second innings, in which on several occasions he had found himself in uncomfortable proximity to the Australian quickie (a man renowned for being able to wolf down a Big Mac in one gulp), he observed that "he was so close you could smell his dodgy breath".

Winner on Points

Hard one to call. Hughes finally ensured Greatbatch's dismissal by extracting his stumps in time-honoured fashion. But Greatbatch had laid a sound foundation for the Kiwi middle-order, enabling them to clinch the game by five wickets in front of a 10,000 last-day crowd, all admitted free, and square the series.

Mike Gatting
v Shakoor Rana
Pakistan v England
2nd Test. Faisalabad. December 1987.

A case of irresistible force meeting immovable object, or, more simply, two short fat blokes getting into a row in the most famous of all examples of rage stopped play. It all started when Gatting tried to move David Capel from deep backward square to a single-saving position closer to the wicket as Eddie Hemmings, completing a (widespread) triangle of short fat blokes, prepared to bowl his off-breaks. (Hemmings, let it be remembered, was immortalised by Australian spectators when they released a pig bearing his name to forage around the Melbourne boundary edge.) Shakoor Rana stopped Hemmings in mid run-up to inform Salim Malik, the batsman, of Gatting's action, and reprimanded the England captain for contravening the spirit of the game. A defiant Gatting maintained that he had done no such thing and, as the language descended to a level that made gutter look the height of literary aspiration, finger wagging at five paces ensued. The following day, Shakoor refused to return until Gatting apologised, the Middlesex man remained stubborn and the third day was lost to frantic behind-the-scenes negotiation.

Winner on Points

Probably Shakoor, even though there remains suspicion that he regarded the stand-off as a defining moment in an officiating career in which his previous form included delaying a Pakistan/India Test by 11 minutes in a dispute with Sunil Gavaskar over a bowler's follow-through, and arguing with Jeremy Coney, the New Zealand skipper, after he turned down an appeal. Gatting was ultimately forced to consume something even he found unpalatable – a large portion of humble pie – but his scribbled note of apology bore the hallmark of a small boy grudgingly forced by his parents into expressing his regret for making rude noises during Mass. "Dear Shakoor Rana," Gatting wrote, "I'm sorry for the bad language used during the second day of the Test in Faisalabad." There is, it transpires, no truth in the rumour that the words "PS: you're still a f***ing cheating b*****d" had to be tippexed out by the England tour management before delivery.

Arjuna Ranatunga
v Ross Emerson
Sri Lanka v England
Triangular tournament. Adelaide. January 1999.

Like Gatting, Arjuna Ranatunga, perhaps Sri Lanka's finest captain, was of somewhat stunted stature, bore a certain rotundity and had a widely-publicised run-in with a foreign umpire. It has never been determined definitively whether his nickname of Napoleon is attributable to these factors or an immutable nature in his leadership. Maybe it was just that the cricket world was threatened with being blown apart after the left-hander said, "not tonight, Ross" when, under the lights at the Adelaide Oval, Emerson, an Australian, called Murali Muralitharan for chucking. In a tactical manoeuvre of which the diminutive 19th century Corsican would have been proud, Ranatunga, incensed because Muralitharan had already been cleared of throwing by the ICC, led his side to the edge of the field where he used all 51 forefinger gestures of which body language experts say man is capable to point out the error of Emerson's ways. It was probably not what Emerson needed, having been absent from his day job for eight weeks on stress leave, and the game only resumed after Ranatunga had mobiled the Sri Lanka chief executive – by coincidence his brother – for further instructions. But the ill-feeling boiled over into the rest of the game, with minor players on both sides getting involved in physical and verbal exchanges.

Winner on Points

Ranatunga. While Emerson was stood down from duty for a Sri Lanka game later that week, Ranatunga used the clever legal argument of his lawyers first to delay a hearing into his behaviour, and then to escape, to many's disgust, with a six month ban, suspended for a year. A year later, the MCC incorporated a section on the Spirit of Cricket into its revision of the Laws of the Game.

Rashid Patel
v Raman Lamba
West Zone v North Zone
Duleep Trophy final. Jamshedpur. January 1991.

Raman Lamba, a talented India batsman of the 1990s, was tragically killed in 1998 after being struck by a ball at short leg, where he had unwisely taken up residence without a helmet. But the suspicion that he would one day come to a sticky end on a cricket field may have been planted some years earlier when an enraged bowler tried to beat him with a stump. The testy nature of the final of the inter-zone competition was already apparent from the number of short-pitched deliveries that had been bowled, so when Lamba, the North Zone batsman, chided Rashid Patel about his length and line, the light on Patel's fuse was some way to reaching its destination. And he showed it as he deliberately ran through the crease and propelled a bouncer at his opponent from about 16 yards. When Lamba protested, Patel finally exploded, scampering to the batsman's end, removing a stump, hitting out at him and non-striker Ajay Jadeja before continuing the fracas by pursuing Lamba down to third man. When Lamba realised he hadn't shaken off the wild-eyed quickie with his tactical retreat to the outfield, he decided the only form of defence was attack and as Patel got within striking distance, he lifted his bat above his head and signalled he was quite willing to give as much as he might be about to receive.

Winner on Points

The bout was abandoned, and with it the match, as the crowd, stirred by events on the field, started throwing stones and bottles over the fencing. Patel and Lamba were later banned from cricket for 13 months and ten months respectively for their roles in the incident. If that result was not quite what Lamba would have wanted, he could at least console himself with the news that North Zone had been awarded the match on first-innings lead.

5

Glenn McGrath
v Ramnaresh Sarwan
West Indies v Australia
4th Test. Antigua. May 2003.

One satellite network supplying this series to the Americas billed the contest as Australian Authority versus Caribbean Charm. Neither was immediately apparent as McGrath and Sarwan almost came to blows on the penultimate day of this match, as the home side rallied towards the record score to win a Test by a team batting second. McGrath, fired by a potent sense of self-righteous indignation after Sarwan's response to his sledging, towered above the West Indies vice-captain in an aggressive exchange of views beamed to impressionable young cricketers around the globe. It had started when McGrath, portrayed off the field as a New Age, caring kind of a bloke, introduced a childishly homophobic element to proceedings by badgering Sarwan for intimate details he suggested the Guyanese batsman had of a certain part of Brian Lara's anatomy. When Sarwan, thinking on his feet, counter-sledged with the recommendation that McGrath's wife would possibly have better knowledge of the subject, the lanky bowler erupted, unleashing a torrent of abuse which, when purged of its liberal peppering of profanities, read: "Mention my wife again and I'll rip your head off." Sarwan's response may have lacked the wit of Eddo Brandes, the Zimbabwean who once responded to a bowler's query as to why he was so fat by quipping that it was because every time he slept with the bowler's wife she gave him a biscuit, but, in its swiftness, it failed to take into account that the New South Wales seamer had missed the first two Tests of the series to remain in Sydney with his seriously ill spouse.

Winner on Points

Sarwan. McGrath was left feeling sheepish when he accepted that the West Indian, a regular dining partner after close of play, had answered spontaneously rather than spitefully. Nevertheless, fuel was added to the fire of controversy when the incident ascended to prime ministerial level, where the Aussie premier John Howard, like most politicians not fully cognisant of the facts, suggested that McGrath's behaviour had been typical of how any proud Australian would have reacted in the circumstances. The more sophisticated of his nation's population were left cringing with embarrassment.

6

Clem Hill v Peter McAlister
New South Wales
Cricket Association offices
Selection meeting. February 1912.

On the eve of a fresh Test series or tour, cricket followers like nothing better than ruminating at length on the make-up of the competing XIs, the respective merits of the opposing players providing the perfect opportunity to slate the selectors. Some of the best disagreements, however, have taken place behind closed doors, although the one at the New South Wales Cricket Association offices in Sydney on the night of February 3, 1912, didn't stay a secret for long. It should, perhaps, have been foreseen that the meeting would degenerate into what The Australasian called 'open rupture', for gathered around a table in the association's headquarters to pick the team for the fourth Test against England were Frank Iredale,

Syd Smith, and, most poignantly, Clem Hill and Peter McAlister. McAlister was an embittered Victorian frustrated by lack of Test opportunities; Hill was a South Australian, and the country's captain who had presided over the 4-1 series victory against the South Africans the previous summer. Hill was still seething over a telegram McAlister had sent him over the selection of the team for the third Test, in which he suggested that the skipper should leave himself out. When McAlister labelled his subsequent captaincy as the worst he had seen in many years, and refused to retract his comments, Hill leant across the table and, depending on which account you believe, 'slapped him gently with an open hand' to indicate he had been 'heckled beyond endurance' or 'landed a severe blow, unawares, under his left eye'. What isn't contested is that an enraged McAlister then raced round the table and pulled Hill from his chair, the grappling pair engaging in a spot of rockstaresque room-demolition that lasted up to 20 minutes and ended with a triumphant Hill standing astride a horizontal, bloodied and bruised McAlister. His point made, Hill dusted himself down and exited the room, and was striding down the corridor when McAlister leapt to his feet and yelled: 'Come back and fight, you coward.'

Winner on Points

Hill's arm raised by the referee. Although he resigned his post as a selector, he was cheered to the wicket in each of his remaining innings of the England series. However, his invitation to tour England later that year was withdrawn because of a dispute with the Australian Board over who should manage the side, and he didn't represent his country again. McAlister, who had caused an outcry three years earlier when, as the first chairman of selectors, he picked himself as vice-captain on the tour to England ahead of worthier candidates, went to his deathbed still proclaiming that the fight would have been more even had Hill 'invited him outside' to settle their differences rather than caught him off guard.*

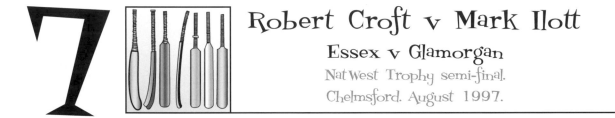

7

Robert Croft v Mark Ilott

Essex v Glamorgan

NatWest Trophy semi-final.
Chelmsford. August 1997.

Wander into the average county cricket ground on a match day and you will find the few spectators, and sometimes a number of players, barely able to raise their eyelids, let alone an interest in the outcome of the game. But a limited-overs cup semi-final is no ordinary day: the public pours in, while players mired in anonymity realise that at stake is their appearance in the end-of-season showpiece at Lord's where, for one day, they can cast off their image as journeymen and pretend they have arrived. No-one, after all, remembers a defeated Gillette, NatWest or C&G Trophy semi-finalist. This would no doubt have been preying on the minds

of Croft and Ilott as their match moved towards its nerve-shattering finalé in the August twilight. The game had already had its fractious moments as Essex chased an improbable 302 to win when Stuart Law, their overseas star, hit on the glove by a high full toss from Darren Thomas, hurled down his bat and uttered a few oaths at the bowler. The innings continued after the Glamorgan players had told him to 'put his rattle and dummy back in the pram'. So when, as the clock ticked round to 8.10pm, and with eight wickets down and six runs required to win, Mark Ilott, a tail-ender, got to the non-striker's end and saw Waqar Younis, the purveyor of blistering, toe-crushing, reverse inswinging yorkers, getting ready to bowl, the tension finally boiled over. Ilott's appeal against the light to the umpires enraged Croft, at mid-off, and as the two players argued about the request, they began pushing and shoving each other in full view of a British television audience, swiftly becoming celebrities as lead items on the BBC and ITV news bulletins.

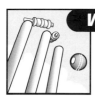

Winner on Points

Well, Ilott got his way and Essex returned the following day to complete their victory. But the bad PR the game

had received overnight meant the pair had to embrace on the field before play to show there was no long-term damage to a friendship which had begun when they played against each other as school-boys. Each was fined £1,000 by his dismayed county, and Ilott complained that the publicity given to the incident had driven his mother to conclude that he was 'an enemy of the state'. Weeks later, the ECB imposed a suspended sentence of two NatWest Trophy matches on the pair. Some observers, however, sought to place ultimate blame on an outside factor: Nasser Hussain, the Essex and England captain who, in an article before the match, had written: 'We need to get a bit of nastiness in our game.'

8

Phil Tufnell v Peter McConnell

Australia v England

2nd Test. Melbourne. January 1991.

We've become accustomed, over the years, to seeing sports stars square up to officials; think Roy Keane's neck, billowing like a bullfrog, as he questions yet another yellow card; think John McEnroe's brattish tirades as he queries another line call at Wimbledon. And how often, when we see this sort of behaviour, do we not wish that the official would for once cast off his aura of superior detachment, and show that he or she too is human by returning some of the abuse, perhaps even giving the noxious upstart a darn good thumping. Peter McConnell, an Australian officiating in this Test, is one who, if his behaviour in this match is to be believed, would subscribe to that approach – and few could really blame him if he had been on the receiving end of one of Phil Tufnell's infamous tantrums. The thing is, he wasn't. The temperamental slow left-armer was on this occasion a picture of innocence when he politely inquired of McConnell how many balls were left in his over and was a little bowled over by the response. "Count 'em yourself, you Pommie c***," McConnell shot back, in six words ensuring Anglo-Aussie relations remained as distant as a Middle East peace settlement.

Winner on Points

Tuffers, on this occasion. While from the boundary edge it looked as if the shocked spinner, making his Test debut, was indulging in some of his usual histrionics, he was merely pointing out to the official that he shouldn't speak to him in such a manner. Graham Gooch, the England captain, had overheard the exchange from his position at mid-off and concurred, walking towards the umpire and delivering his own rebuke – a show of solidarity so surprising to Tufnell that he recorded in his autobiography that "you could have tied my tits together with candyfloss".

Viv Richards v Allan Border and Steve Rixon

Australia v West Indies

5th Test. Sydney. December 1984/January 1985.

The master blaster, the sobriquet attached to the West Indian as his unique talents became increasingly apparent, was no stranger to controversy, one incident in his early days nearly putting an end to his career before it had started. Granted a half-day off to watch their prodigy in action for Antigua, islanders reacted angrily when Richards refused to accept a first-ball dismissal and stood at the crease banging his bat on the ground. His supporters invaded the outfield shouting, "no Vivi, no match", forcing the players off for two hours. After the delay, Richards was given a mistaken impression of his own importance when he was reinstated,

only to be stumped for another nought. (A subsequent nought in the second innings made him probably the only player to record three ducks in a match.) The authorities showed their muscle in due course, though, when a committee of inquiry suspended the 17-year-old from all cricket for two years. Forced to express his sporting prowess away from the cricket field, he found an outlet in boxing, probably unaware that his experience would come in handy several years later on a tour to Australia, when he invited the home side's captain, Allan Border, and wicketkeeper Steve Rixon round to the back of the pavilion for some fisticuffs at the end of play, after an exchange of views about a rejected appeal. Only the intervention of the media, who hurried to the respective dressing-rooms at the close, prevented the scheduled bout actually taking place.

Winner on Points

Rixon and Border, but they had, in effect, nobbled the jury. In the days before the implementation of ICC match referees, Graeme Wood, the Australia vice-captain, and team-mates Kepler Wessels and Andrew Hilditch were appointed to hear the charges against the pair, unsurprisingly exonerating them of using bad language. But they raised the stakes by suggesting that Richards had been unable to control his tongue. Wes Hall, the West Indies manager, was incensed and while agreeing that his batsman had not been "at Sunday School that afternoon", the report's implication that the Australians were innocent bystanders cut little ice. Nonetheless, Hall aimed at reconciliation, but his contention that there had "always been a warmth and harmony between our two peoples" which should not be tarnished by "one or two delinquents" did not bear scrutiny in a series which had grown ever more discordant.

10

Dennis Lillee
v Javed Miandad

Australia v Pakistan

1st Test, Perth, November 1981.

The year 2003 produced a number of events worthy of documentation in the cricketing archives, not least of which was the publication within months of each other of the autobiographies of Dennis Lillee – his third – and Javed Miandad. This happy coincidence was to allow connoisseurs of cricket conflict to indulge in a fascinating retrospective, from the standpoints of both protagonists, of one of the finest examples of the genre to have been captured on film, videotape and in the columns of esteemed journals the world over. When these two most volatile of characters clashed in Perth, it produced a confrontation of truly comic-strip proportions, Miandad obliging in playing Gnasher to Lillee's Dennis the Menace. Unusually, though, the incident came not at a crucial moment in a close and tense game when players' emotions, stretched to breaking point, are understandably liable to be put on public parade, but at a time when Australia had assumed comfortable control of proceedings on the fourth afternoon at the Waca. Miandad played a ball down to fine leg and, as he ran the single, found Lillee in his path. Lillee made a remark about Miandad's luck and turned to go back to his mark. According to the bowler, Miandad poked him in the ribs as he passed, so he tried to grab him, missed and followed up by trying to stick his boot up the Pakistani's backside, an action described as everything from a "vicious killer blow" to a "karate kick". Miandad's own fiery nature led him to respond, raising his bat above his head and threatening to hit the Aussie before the pair were separated by umpire Tony Crafter.

Winner on Points

Miandad. He got off scot-free, while Lillee was fined $200 by his fellow players who sat in judgment. The umpires were not happy with the extent of Lillee's punishment and, after they complained, he was called before an Australian Cricket Board adjudicator. The bowler claimed to have video footage from a previously unseen angle which showed Miandad whacking him as he went by, but was scuppered when he found the VCR was broken. He was suspended for two matches.

65

11

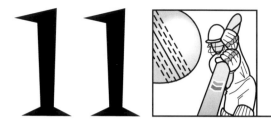

Brian Lara
v Dermot Reeve
Northamptonshire v Warwickshire
County Championship. Northampton. June 1994.

A newspaper columnist once tried to draw a comparison between Brian Lara and Mozart, not so much because the left-hander's flow of runs matched the Austrian composer's prodigious musical output but rather because he risked following the virtuoso in cracking up under the strain of his own genius. But while Wolfgang Amadaeus had a small family to support and had to pawn his belongings to survive, Brian Charles was able to employ two business managers to take care of his expanding empire. It is little surprise, then, that

Dermot Reeve, the Trinidadian's captain during his season at Warwickshire in 1994, would have been hard-pushed to see the parallels had they been pointed out to him. Especially when Lara's simmering lack of respect for Reeve's authority reached a discordant crescendo in late June, the world's best batsman directing a torrent of invective at his skipper that would have embarrassed a Gangsta Rap lyricist. The outburst occurred after Reeve had urged Lara to contain his displeasure at a decision by umpire Alan Jones. While Reeve, who later described it as the worst example of player indiscipline he had witnessed, tried to maintain a semblance of self-control in front of his team, pointing out to Lara that he was in danger of becoming a prima donna (though, depending on which version you believe, possibly not as politely as that), the West Indies superstar pointed to his knee and ran off the field for treatment. He spent the next day of the match resting under the dressing-room table, only occasionally stirring himself to ask the score.

Winner on Points

Unquestionably Lara. Although Reeve complained that he was being undermined, Warwickshire officials, desperate to continue cashing in on Lara's pulling power, urged him to dance to Lara's theme, even going so far as to suggest he should ring his overseas player to apologise. Reeve later discovered that Lara's antipathy was brought about by his belief that the Warwickshire captain had originally wanted an all-rounder to replace Allan Donald as their overseas player.

12  Twelfth Man
Inzamam-ul-Haq v Shiv Kumar Thind.

Skating is a pastime both gentle and artistic in nature – although Nancy Kerrigan, who was once clubbed on the knee by associates of her US Olympic arch rival Tonya Harding, may disagree; curling also so, the nearest the sport getting to savagery being when two team members take to scrubbing the ice to within an inch of its life as the stone is propelled across its surface. So it was inevitable, really, that the most significant confrontation at the Toronto Cricket, Skating and Curling club would involve the first of these sports. The club had attempted to break the ice in Pakistani-Indian relations by staging the annual Sahara Cup one-day series on neutral territory. However, no thaw was evident, the meeting of the Asian rivals conversely continuing to show its propensity for raising temperatures, especially when one spectator, Thind, an Indian living in the Canadian city, decided to roundly abuse – should that be abuse the rounded – Inzamam, from the sidelines, continuously voicing his opinion, via megaphone, that the Pakistani resembled a particularly substantial dish of Bombay Aloo. Thind had already picked up on Salim Malik's likeness to the Buddha without creating undue offence, but, to be fair, being compared to a plate of curried potato is less flattering than being bracketed with a man who inspired a world faith. Nevertheless, a short period of meditation would have probably benefited Inzamam who instead jumped into the stand to challenge Thind. When his abuser threw his megaphone at him, Inzamam borrowed a bat from the team's twelfth man and tried to hoist the Indian over mid-wicket before being restrained and escorted to the pavilion to cool down. The match was stopped for 37 minutes, by which time Thind had reported Inzamam to the Toronto police. Two days later, Inzamam counter-filed for assault, but peace was restored when both complainants agreed to drop the charges. Inzamam, though, was fined and banned for two matches by the Pakistan management.

69

Chapter Four

The Worst Mistakes

The Worst Mistakes

It would be wrong to give the impression that umpires bear sole responsibility for the misfortunes that befall those who take part in the world's most merciless sport. Funny, but wrong. In fairness, it has to be said that there is no monopoly on stupidity, no single cause of the errors that pervade the game. The phrase 'flannelled fools' wasn't coined for nothing, even if nowadays players are more likely to be dressed in lycra. Barely a day goes by without someone making an idiot of himself on the pitch, in the dressing-room, in a press conference or in front of the word processor. And what's more, nobody seems to learn.

1

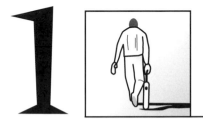

Harry Makepeace

Sussex v Lancashire

County Championship. Eastbourne. July 1907.

Scorers, it is widely believed, are rather inadequate creatures, notable mainly for their incredibly small, neat handwriting and unfeasibly large collections of coloured pens. They beaver away in the hinterland of the game, unloved and barely noticed – until they do something wrong. It doesn't matter how many fancy geometric charts they have prepared, they will not easily be forgiven. Especially if you believe you have just reached your maiden century in first-class cricket, allowing your captain to make an immediate declaration, only to find that they have mistakenly attributed a leg bye to your score and have to readjust their records. This was what happened in this game to JWH 'Harry' Makepeace, who discovered that he had acknowledged the crowd for a rather splendid 99 not out. He had to wait four more seasons to record his first official century.

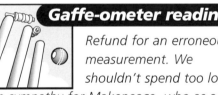

Gaffe-ometer reading

Refund for an erroneous measurement. We shouldn't spend too long on sympathy for Makepeace, who as a footballer with Everton played in two FA Cup finals – one earlier that year – and gained four caps for England. He also went on to play four Tests for his country, and ended his career with a haul of 42 first-class centuries.

2

Francis Allan
Australia v England
1st Test. Melbourne. March 1877.

Contemporary Australian teams have displayed such depth of talent and consistency that the average Test hopeful might think he has to crawl across the Nullabor desert in order to have a chance of catching the selectors' eyes. And back. Naked. But places in the national side were not always at such a premium, as Francis Allan, a mainstay of the Victoria attack in the late 19th century would testify if he was still around to do so. Allan, a left arm opening bowler who laced his fast medium deliveries with disconcertingly late swing, showed such indifference to his country's cricket that he wrote himself straight out of the history books by declining to lead the Australian bowling in the first ever Test match in favour of a previous engagement at the Warrnambool Agricultural Show.

Gaffe-ometer reading

Moderate. Unlike Michael Slater, Greg Blewett and Stuart Law, among many others, his time was to come again. Not that he made the most of it. Touring England the following summer, he found the weather not to his liking and 25 wickets in 15 matches was a meagre return for a man dubbed, perhaps a tad prematurely, Bowler of the Century. Back in the warmer climes of Melbourne, he made his one and only Test appearance in England's tour in 1878–9 before retiring from the first-class game to take a job in the Victoria Lands Department in his beloved Warrnambool.

3

Hugh Thurlow
Australia v South Africa
4th Test. Adelaide. 1932.

Some players are destined never to make their mark on history through their own deeds; like desperate rock band groupies, they must be content with hanging on to the coattails of celebrity. So it was with Hugh Thurlow, a lively roundish-armed pace bowler who played 30 times for Queensland. A chemist by profession, he was unable to alchemise a wicket in his debut Test match at the Adelaide Oval - a fast bowler's graveyard at the time. However, when it was his turn to bat, he perhaps imagined that he had awakened some dark forces. Australia were 499-9 when he arrived at the crease to partner Don Bradman, and he stuck around long enough to help the great man edge towards his triple century. However, with just one run required of the master, Thurlow managed to get himself run out.

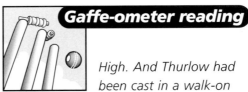

Gaffe-ometer reading

High. And Thurlow had been cast in a walk-on role in the Bradman Summer Special once before. In 1929, in a Sheffield Shield game between Queensland and NSW, he bowled the delivery which Bradman dispatched to the mid-wicket boundary to pass Bill Ponsford's world record individual score of 437. He never played Test cricket again.

4

Mike Atherton
South Africa v England
World Cup group match. Rawalpindi. 1996.

While an obsessive and frankly unhealthy interest in the minutiae of metatarsals (injured or not) is a helpful qualification for a successful sports journalist, of greater significance is the ability to criticise, on the slightest pretext, those from whom they effectively derive their living. However, the thick skin that most of them parade to the world can prove surprisingly easy to penetrate when the roles are reversed and their own shortcomings are pointed out to them, as Mike Atherton,who never suffered reporters gladly, found to his cost after his side had suffered a 78-run defeat in this match. Frustrated by the faltering English of the Pakistan Press Association's Asghar Ali during the post-match press conference, his aside calling for "someone to get this buffoon out of here" backfired spectacularly. While the English contingent raced gleefully to their keyboards to send word of their national captain's latest faux pas back to base, the Pakistanis went into an over-drive of outrage; so much so that even when the finest minds in the England camp combined to draft a 25-word apology and convey it through John Barclay, the assistant manager, the World Cup hosts were by no means satisfied. Rawalpindi's Sports Journalists' Association demanded a "proper apology", invoking any number of examples to show just how very peeved they were. "Whether it was a journalist, the captain of Pakistan, the groundsman or the Prime Minister himself," a spokesman raged, "Atherton has insulted a person trying to do his job. I would have thought that it would have occurred to an intelligent man with an honours degree from Cambridge that the journalist was not speaking in his mother tongue."

Gaffe-ometer reading

High. Atherton, not the most jocular captain of modern times, apparently meant his remark to lighten proceedings. His gag writer was sacked on the spot.

Roy Marshall

Hampshire v Glamorgan

County Championship. Bournemouth. June 1969.

The rain had finally relented; the umpires had inspected and the groundstaff had hurried around, busily mopping up the few remaining damp patches on the outfield. The Glamorgan players jogged gently from the pavilion, their captain, Tony Lewis, directing them to their positions in the rich choral tones of the Valleys which befitted a man whose musical ability had once seen him perform on the violin for the Welsh National Youth Orchestra. Another Tone – Cordle – prepared to resume battle, the medium-quick bowler measuring out his run-up and scraping his boot across the place where he intended to start from. A team-mate tossed him the ball, freshly buffed up on one side, and Cordle placed his second and third fingers at a slight, but precise, angle across the seam. He looked down at his feet and then looked up, focusing his eyes on the portion of the pitch where he intended to land his first delivery. Lloyd Budd, the umpire at the bowler's end, dropped his arm and gave the order to "Play". Unfortunately, they couldn't, because there was no batsman: the Hampshire team had left early, believing that the umpires had abandoned play for the day.

Gaffe-ometer reading

One journalist had seen Roy Marshall, the captain, and his troops, "leave, changed and off to the next engagement" at around 4pm as he sat in the pavilion "contemplating a flat beer". But he was in no doubt where the blame lay, suggesting that Marshall had been misled by a rumour started by "the well-meaning busybodies one finds at county grounds" which had filtered through to the dressing-room.

6

Mark Boucher
South Africa v Sri Lanka
World Cup group match. Durban. March 2003.

O ne of the discoveries that air crash experts routinely make in their investigations into major accidents is that there is no single cause; rather, there is a chain of events leading to the disaster and if just one link in the sequence could have been broken, there would have been no ultimate catastrophe. Those casting their eyes over the wreckage of the Rainbow Nation's fall to earth, at the group stage of the World Cup they spent five years organising, might have come to the same conclusion. *If only* it hadn't rained, forcing reliance on the complicated Duckworth/Lewis system for weather-affected one-day matches; *if only* the South African management hadn't misinterpreted that system to mean that the total given at the end of each over was that for a win and not a tie; *if only*, when they realised their mistake and sent twelfth man Nicky Boje out to update the batsmen, umpire Steve Bucknor had not waved him off; *if only* Mark Boucher, the batsman on strike, had taken that single off the final ball of Muttiah Muralitharan's over – the 45th – instead of patting it carefully to mid-wicket in the mistaken belief that his team had reached their reduced target; *if only* just one of those events could have been changed, South Africa, one run from an outright victory when a saturated Bucknor ordered the players off, would have taken four points instead of the two they got for the tie and would have made it to the Super Sixes (instead of New Zealand) – and then who knows what?

Gaffe-ometer reading

Massive. As the South Africans sat gloomily in the dressing room, praying that the rain would eventually relent and they would be able to return and rectify matters, an embarrassed Boucher was quite possibly thinking: if only I hadn't punched the air in triumph after hitting Muralitharan's penultimate ball for six.

81

7 Ted Dexter and Bob Willis

England. 1985

Holding, Marshall, Garner... Pringle, Allott, Sidebottom. Spot the difference? One lot was lightning fast, liable to shatter bones and reputations, the other bunch the medium side of military, with silly names. Batsmen died, or batsmen died laughing. In an attempt to halt English cricket bearing the continued brunt of Caribbean cockiness, two former captains of the national side put their heads together and almost came up with an idea. Deciding to fight fire with fire, they persuaded a Yorkshire brewery to stump up the readies to finance a countrywide search for a new Trueman and Snow to spearhead an assault on a few West Indian knuckles of their own, in a kind of pilot version of *Cricket Idol*. However, they chose to focus their search not on those with a basic understanding of the rudiments of their craft – in this case a bouncer and a long stare – turning their sights instead to natural athletes who had never so much as gripped a cherry in anger. The press and the public were infected with enthusiasm for the scheme; 3,000 applicants were whittled down to 600 for trials; six made up the final Websters squad and, of these, four were voted off, leaving the chosen two...

Gaffe-ometer reading

It was bound to end in tears. Well, do you remember that classic series of 1986 in which Tom Stancombe and David Dismore reduced the West Indies to quivering wrecks on their home turf? Me neither.

8

Peter May

England v West Indies. June to August. 1988.

Athletes may not, ultimately, have been enough to rescue England from a pace pasting in 1985/86, but the participants of track and field provide a fitting metaphor for the extraordinary goings-on three years later, when the West Indies next toured. Under the stewardship of Peter May, a great batsman but a rather less convincing chairman of selectors, the country went through a complete 4 x 100 metres relay team of captains. The first 100 was encouraging, Mike Gatting being quick out of the blocks to end a sequence of ten defeats against their Caribbean opponents with a draw at Trent Bridge, only for it to be ruled a false start because of his off-field activities (see chapter 10). The baton was passed to John Emburey, who failed to clear either of the hurdles at Lord's and Old Trafford and was promptly dropped. May next played his nepotistic hand, plucking his godson Chris Cowdrey from the practice track with the words: "His style of leadership is what is now required." Needless to say, it wasn't, the West Indies winning by ten wickets at Headingley in a game that only made it to the third day because the drainage system failed. Cowdrey was dispatched to the high jump as Graham Gooch assumed responsibility for the last leg at the Oval, but he failed to make it to the finish line when he dislocated his finger in the West Indies' second innings, forcing Derek Pringle to puff his way to the tape.

Gaffe-ometer reading

May dug himself ever more deeply into the pit reserved for the worst selectors, piling error upon blunder upon clanger upon boob until he hit a major pipeline and sparked a huge explosion propelling him for ever more from the ranks of cricket officialdom.

9

Bertie Buse
Somerset v Lancashire
County Championship. Bath. July 1953.

Cricket lovers have shown their admiration for their heroes in a variety of ways, although Syd Gregory, an Australian Test player of the late 1800s and early 1900s, was no doubt taken aback when, batting for New South Wales at the SCG, an appreciative spectator rushed out and laid an enormous marrow at his feet. If he appeared ungrateful, it was probably because he'd have preferred some hard currency, his partners in a city sports store having defrauded him some years earlier and left him bankrupt. Gregory did ultimately get a testimonial which garnered a tidy sum, but the system which allows players to supplement their meagre salaries by way of a glorified tip has become something of an anachronism in an age when moderate performances can earn you a winter's income from punditry in the Sky studios. There was no such option in the days of Bertie Buse, a Somerset all-rounder. Given the chance in 1953, after 24 years of service, to build a nest-egg for his life outside the game, he designated the county championship encounter with Lancashire, at the start of the popular Bath Festival, as his benefit match. Unwisely, though, he had failed to study the history of battles between the counties; if he had, he might have noticed they had practically created a template for one-day cricket years before anyone had seriously entertained the concept. Three times the two had completed a two-innings match within the first day, and by 5.34pm on the Monday at Bath, they had done it again, leaving Buse to contemplate the bare stands and his equally empty pockets for the remaining couple of days. Not that Buse could lay the blame entirely elsewhere, his figures of 6–41 in Lancashire's innings of 158 contributing to his own shortfall.

Gaffe-ometer reading

Buse found it really wasn't his week, in both a financial and a bowling sense, claiming only one of the 18 wickets that fell later on the first day of the festival's next match against Kent. He did finally strike it lucky in the second innings, hitting an impressive hundred that was instrumental in his team's eventual victory, but by then the collecting cap was no longer doing the rounds.

10 Ivo Bligh and the Ashes

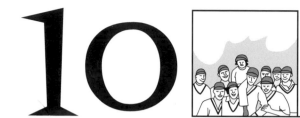

Melbourne. Kent and Lords. 1883-1982

The Ashes are one of the most recognisable trophies in sport – if trophy is a fitting description for a little urn – something about which even those with only a passing interest in the national game are likely to be at least vaguely aware. Most of these people, if pushed, would probably have some familiarity with their origins, too – the satirical notices bewailing the death of English cricket that appeared in newspapers after the Australians had beaten England for the first time in this country at the Oval in 1882, and the notion that bails were burnt to mark the event. That the urn, under lock and key in the Lord's museum, is filled with the actual remnants of the cremated bails has never, however, been proved. However, a story that emerged in the 1980s certainly casts doubt over the authenticity of the contents. Wisden, the cricketing bible, had long held the opinion that the Ashes came into being the year after the historic defeat in Australia, when some women at a dinner for the touring Englishmen presented the remains to the Hon. Ivo Bligh, the visiting captain, as a joke. Bligh, who was to become the heriditary peer Lord Darnley, later married one of the donors, Florence Morphy, moving to Cobham Hall, his estate in Kent. After his death in 1927, his wife gave the urn and its contents to the MCC. However, in 1982, a former butler at Cobham Hall came forward to report that a housemaid had once told him that, while cleaning, she had knocked over the "the urn/vase thing that stands on his mantelpiece in Lordship's room" and, finding it full of old ash, had given it "a good clean out and polish before putting it back".

Gaffe-ometer reading

The butler, knowing the true worth of the container, was forced to murmur some choice phrases before getting down on his hands and knees to scrape some wood ash from the fireplace, scoop it into the urn, and return the container to its resting place. Lord Darnley, the MCC and the cricketing public remained none the wiser. Ashes, then, but probably not as we've come to think of them.

11

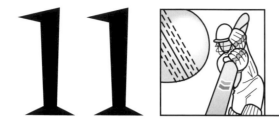

Lance Klusener
South Africa v Sri Lanka
World Cup semi-final. Edgbaston. June 1999.

Allan Donald, South Africa's last man in, was almost run out off the penultimate ball of this heart-stopping semi-final, which would have condemned his country to another near-miss in the competition. Fortunately, he managed to scamper back into his ground at the non-striker's end before calling for a mid-pitch chat with partner Lance Klusener, whose 31 off 15 balls had left South Africa needing just one run to win off the remaining three deliveries. His advice was simple and to the point: "Wait for the right ball, pick your spot and hit it," he said, a request that should not have been too hard to fulfil for a man with a scoring rate of over 90 in the one-day arena, but pressure can do some funny things to a man. Instead of clobbering Damien Fleming over the single-saving field for four like he had done with the first two deliveries, he panicked, and going against his aggressive nature, not to mention Donald's tip, tried to sneak the one to mid off. Donald watched Mark Waugh move in to field and as the ball was returned to the bowler, he was stunned to turn back and find Klusener standing by his side. Adjusting as quickly as he could to the situation, Donald belatedly started to run towards the other end, but Fleming's careful underarm along the pitch to Adam Gilchrist was too quick for him.

Gaffe-ometer reading

Another in a lengthening list of South African World Cup disasters, the resulting tie let Australia in to the final by the back door. What's more, South Africa could have ended Australia's interest in the competition five days earlier, when only Steve Waugh's 120 from 110 balls in their Super Six stage encounter had rescued them.

12  Twelfth Man

A variety of qualities are required of a tour manager, although it is unlikely that the awareness of the cargo capacity of the world's airlines has generally been one of them. That it might need to be for future excursions into the more obscure quarters of the international cricket kingdom was made clear as events unfolded, or, in this case, didn't unfold, in front of 15,000 spectators who had packed into the Jamshedpur stadium on a fine October morning in 1984. Disconcerted to be informed that the one-day international between India and Australia could not make a prompt start because of residual dampness in the pitch, they grew more restive as lunch came and went with no significant activity, and angry when they were told in mid-afternoon that there was no longer time for a full match to take place, and, instead, a "beer" match would be played. When the anger found a physical outlet and the first of several missiles was thrown on to the outfield, panicked officials, fearing a full-blown riot, backed down and agreed a match of 24 overs per side could go ahead. What the crowd had been unaware of was the frenzy of activity taking place behind the scenes and the reason for the delaying tactics: the teams had been unable to take the field because their whites and equipment had not arrived. Officials had been unable to load them on to the same tiny Fokker aircraft the players had been switched

to at Calcutta when it was realised that the airport at Jamshedpur was too small to take bigger jets. It was hastily arranged for the baggage to be transported by van, but the vehicle got held up at the State border and then by heavy traffic. If the crowd thought their troubles were over once play got under way, they were quickly disabused of the notion; the first light spots of rain that fell on the Indian opening batsmen swiftly turned into something more substantial, the teams were led off and the game abandoned. They had seen just 5.1 overs for their money.

Chapter Five

Worst Riots and Crowd Disturbances

Worst Riots and Crowd Disturbances

A correspondent of a famous British national newspaper once suggested that cricket was the best antidote to hooliganism, confidently asserting that a yob invariably "deserts his gang" as soon as he takes to the game "in earnest". What this social reformer failed to note was that rather than deserting his gang for cricket, such "highly-strung creatures" were likely to take them to the cricket, where they diverted their "rampant nervous energy" into channels that he would have regarded as totally inappropriate - lager, gambling and raucous chanting. Nothing much has changed on that score since he authored the piece early in the last century, except that the cricket world has widened, giving us a view of "hooligans" from a variety of cultures. Not that all loudmouths at cricket have been a bad thing; Stephen Gascoigne was a legendary barracker on the Sydney Hill during the 1920s and 30s, his witticisms earning him a 400-word tribute in *The Oxford Companion to Australian Cricket* and a letter of acknowledgment from Jack Hobbs after the great batsman's final Test. Unfortunately, though, few barrackers since, from the wag at the WACA imploring a batsman to "'ave a go you mug", to the football shirted oik to be found at Old Trafford singing "Lanky-Lanky-Lanky-Lanky-Lanc-a-shire" during the summer break from the Premiership, have had Gascoigne's droll wit and sheer understanding of the game. Still, it is comforting to know that misbehaviour among spectators is not the preserve of one country, being experienced at venues as far apart as Peshawar and Port-of-Spain, in enclosures as distant as Headingley's Western Terrace and Melbourne's Bay 13. And it would be too simple to lay the blame purely at the feet of the paying public's Bacchanalian excesses. There are far more complex forces at work, as, from the worst examples of this category, we shall see...

1

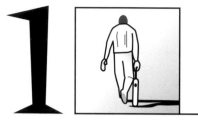

New South Wales v England

Tour match. Sydney. January 1879.

Master criminals, like the greatest batsmen, are distinguished by the precision of their timing. It is perhaps why, alongside Don Bradman, Ned Kelly ranks as the foremost of Australian heroes. The bushranger was certainly on the ball on the second day of England's match against New South Wales at the SCG. While the majority of the state police force was otherwise engaged trying to stop hundreds of spectators continuing a series of threatening pitch invasions, he and his gang galloped into the nearby town of Jerildie, rounded up the remaining bobbies, and herded them into the cells of their own nick before nipping up the road to rob the bank. The initial encroachments had been provoked partly by state rivalries. Lord Harris, the England captain, had engaged George Coulthard, a Victorian, as a travelling umpire and when he ruled that Billy Murdoch, a local favourite, had been run out, these rivalries found their utmost expression (although there is evidence that they were stirred up by bookmakers who had exposed themselves to heavy losses). Up to 3,000 spectators leapt over the boundary fence and swarmed to the middle, surrounding the England players and calling for Coulthard to be removed. As the tourists tried to slip off to the pavilion, one intruder grabbed Harris and started to whip him with a stick. Only the swift intervention of Albert Hornby, the team's featherweight opening batsman who earlier in the tour had shown his appetite for uneven contests by jumping into a Melbourne boxing ring to spar with Jem Mac, the English heavyweight

champion, prevented the nobility from suffering irreparable damage.

Larrikin level

High. Kelly would have been proud of such insubordination. England eventually reached safety, but then the two captains argued over Coulthard's suitability for his role, Harris refused to back down. When Coulthard took the field again, another invasion ensued. A further pavilion conference was convened but, again, England stood by their chosen umpire and when play finally resumed, a hardcore of 300 repossessed the playing area, remaining there until the close.

West Indies v England

2nd Test. Jamaica. February 1968.

It is common to think of hot air as a substance expelled by politicians in such quantities that it could sustain Sir Richard Branson on a continuous circumnavigation of the globe in his hi-tech balloon; it is less common to find incidences when, conversely, it has served to silence them. But that was just what happened on the the fourth afternoon of this match when tear-gas released by the police in a misguided attempt to quell misconduct in the stands floated over the back of the stadium and rendered the Speaker of the nearby Jamaican Parliament, well... speechless. The trouble had begun after Basil Butcher had been given out caught down the leg-side by England wicketkeeper Jim Parks with the West Indies still 29 adrift of saving the follow-on. Butcher's shake of the head at his dismissal was more in frustration at the misbehaviour of a rapidly deteriorating pitch than a display of dissent at the umpire's decision, but it was not seen as such by those furthest from the action, who proceeded to launch empty spirit bottles on to the outfield. The respective captains, Garry Sobers and Colin Cowdrey, went to the site of the disruption and worked to calm the crowd by assuring them Butcher had been fairly caught, but just as peace seemed to have been restored, a police riot squad undid all the good work by racing to the fence and spraying the contents of their noxious canisters into the crowd. The action created a panic-ridden stampede in which women and children were among those lucky to escape serious injury, although there was plentiful coughing, spluttering, trampling and no small measure of vomiting to keep the emergency services busy.

Larrikin level

More rum deal than ruffians. While the recently retired Conrad Hunte sought to blame the disorder on a hardcore rallied by "forces outside cricket", the sports editor of island newspaper The Gleaner criticised the police for failing to get in amongst the crowd to subdue the missile-throwing. Clement Freud, writing in The Sun, preferred to focus on the physical abilities of the local populace, observing: "it is a measure of Jamaican cricket prowess that many of the bottles thrown travelled 70 yards or more."

3

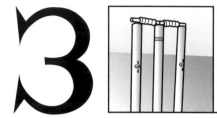

England v Pakistan
One-day international. Edgbaston. May 1987.

Whatever your view of the police in this country, there is something curiously comforting about their ability, with their monotone approach to the English language, to make the most serious of situations seem incredibly mundane. Annoying as it may seem when they've stopped you late at night to inform you that your left rear light is flickering, their unemotional stance serves a higher purpose. Thus, when Mohammed Riaz, a Pakistan supporter, had his jugular vein severed by a flying wine carafe, WPC Teresa Sharpies, having saved his life by stemming the blood flow until an ambu-

lance arrived, told reporters, disappointed in their pursuit of the killer quote: "I was walking along the perimeter boundary when a man came up to me and said 'excuse me officer, my throat seems to have been cut'." But while WPC Sharpies, whose undemonstrative response to probably the ugliest incident at a cricket match in England quite rightly got her hailed as a heroine, her colleagues at Edgbaston were taking no little flak for failing to halt a series of pitch invasions, mainly at the fall of English wickets in a game which would decide the destination of the Texaco Trophy. As the terrace battles between English fans – a couple of them brandishing National Front banners – and their Pakistani counterparts worsened, the boys and girls in blue were forced to call for reinforcements to separate the warring parties. Fifty supporters were eventually ejected and 16 arrested.

Larrikin level

High. Even when England completed a tense one-wicket victory, the trouble didn't stop. The Pakistan team tried to make *a dash for their bus, but when two of them, Ijaz Ahmed and Mohsin Kamal, became separated from the main group, they allegedly used a bat on their own supporters to make their escape – an accusation hotly denied by the tourists' manager. Away from the ground, Ian Botham found himself in an uncomfortable position as he sat in his car in a traffic jam and a group of Pakistan supporters drew level with him. After an exchange of views, he got out of his vehicle and was assaulted by a man with a stump. He later recommended the use of the cat o' nine tails on wayward cricket supporters.*

West Indies v England

3rd Test. Guyana. February/March 1954.

Yorkshiremen have always taken pride in their unyielding natures, especially when it comes to cricket. There was Brian Close, a man who never really thought he'd been in a game unless he had the seam imprint on his forehead to prove it. Or Geoff Boycott, a man whose stubborn occupation of the crease made the Rock of Gibraltar appear simplicity itself to dislodge. Or Ray Illingworth, so convinced that if you want something doing you have to do it yourself that he recalled himself to captain the side in his fifties. This obstinacy of a county which became the last to open its doors to players from outside its boundaries (and fielded ten

professionals at a time when the sport was almost wholly amateur-based) was perfectly reflected in the title of one author's account of the team's approach to the game: *We Don't Play for Fun*. Not that this trait should be seen one-sidedly as negative. Far from it. Take Sir Len Hutton, for example. A batsman matchless in adapting his approach to the needs of the situation, he could be either abstemiously defensive or indulgently flamboyant. This pragmatism came particularly useful during this Test. Hutton, having little faith in the local umpires after a tour game in Georgetown earlier in the trip, had requested that two others be flown in from neighbouring islands to officiate. When the crowd, fuelled by rumours of Hutton's action, saw Clifford McWatt, the Guyanese wicketkeeper, given run out by one of the replacement officials, they erupted, a barrage of bottles, boxes and tins raining down in the direction of square leg. The Guyanese Cricket Board Secretary, Ken Wishart, phoned police, who deployed a helmeted unit armed with tear gas and truncheons, while the Cricket Board chief, WS Jones, braved the assault to go on to the field and implore Hutton to come off. It was then that Hutton delivered a classic riposte which is written in the annals of Yorkshire folklore. "No thanks," he said, "we want a couple more wickets tonight."

Larrikin level

Medium. Georgetown's daily newspapers turned inwards on themselves, describing the crowd's behaviour as, at one extreme, an understated "breach of good manners" to, at the other, a hyperbolic "mob rule in the jaws of hell". Hutton, no doubt, saw it as little more excitable than the average Yorkshire committee meeting, and his perversity paid off as Jim Laker immediately snaffled Sonny Ramadhin and England went on to win by nine wickets.

5

TOTAL **5**

West Indies XI
v Australia XI

World Series Cricket 4th Supertest.
Guyana. March 1979.

While most cricket watchers are stoically prepared by experience for rain or bad light to stop or delay play, for others it can cause great dismay as they scour the skies for the most distant cumulus nimbus or sit on tenterhooks anticipating the imminent illumination of the the third of those infuriating lamps on the scoreboard light meter. Some will bemoan the fact that their own clubs invariably play in far worse conditions, others will lean over the boundary surrounds and prod the turf disapprovingly with their golf umbrellas. Those who haven't adjourned to the nearest bar, though, will watch with growing incredulity as the teams proceed to warm up on a supposedly drenched outfield while the umpires agree to "look again" in an hour. At this point a minority will take the law into their own hands. Like the specatator in Guyana who appointed himself judge, jury and human heavy roller, making for the middle, lying down in the popping crease and rumbling up and down the uncovered pitch for several minutes to provide definitive proof of its lack of moisture to the rest of the crowd. It was the kind of action liable to provoke a riot – and it did. To be fair, the crowd had been sitting patiently since 1pm in expectation of a prompt start after a West Indies Cricket Board official's comments in the previous day's paper. When, at 2pm, the umpires declared play could still not start for another hour and a half, the bottles started flying. One hit the main stand clock, which stopped, never to go again. Spectators burst through the fences, ransacking the pavilion and bar – one making off with the cash register – while players retreated into their dressing-rooms, fortifying themselves with helmets and bats for protection, before the application of tear gas created the opening for a guard of armed police to rush the teams to their respective buses.

Larrikin level

Off the scale. This riot has been described by some observers as the worst in cricket history; Desmond Haynes, the West Indies opener, would no doubt concur after seeking refuge behind the locked door of a dressing-room toilet cubicle – only to find an armed policeman cowering alongside him.

6

Holland V England

World Cup group match. Peshawar.

February 1996.

The Pakistan frontier town of Peshawar is not a place for the faint-hearted. When Marco Polo passed through in 1275 he found a people who "worship idols and have an evil disposition", though the explorer probably delayed making that observation till he was safely back in Italy. The tourist board's literature, which highlights the area's undoubted scenic charms, goes to pains to reassure would-be visitors that they have done away with the penchant for idolatry since converting to Islam. But English cricket journalists covering the World Cup in 1996 remained unconvinced by its additional claims to 'legendary hospitality", noting that while hotel guests were requested not to enter their accommodation

108

with firearms, no such demand was made of spectators attending this group match in the town. Perhaps this is what enabled one man to enter the ground and aim a small spear with a nail driven through it at Darren Gough as he fielded near the boundary.

Larrikin level

Potentially High. Had Gough not had the wherewithal to avoid

reacting a la Sylvester Clarke (see chapter 2) it is likely he would still be taking a long hike back to Leeds via a big kick up the Khyber Pass. Instead, he enjoyed safe passage to the next England game by simply reporting the occurrence to umpire KT Francis, and the man responsible for propelling the weapon was arrested. Nevertheless, the Yorkshire paceman's captain, Michael Atherton, safely out of range at extra cover, was not unduly sympathetic to his strike bowler. "It was all meant in good spirit," he suggested.

7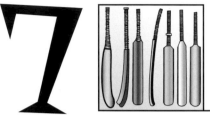

New Zealand v Australia
2nd Test. Auckland. February/March 1977

August 5, 1975 will be marked down as a significant day if or when an illustrated history is ever produced about the varieties of spectator that have passed through the hallowed surrounds of the home of cricket; no, it wasn't the date that an MCC member who'd been sitting very quietly in the Lord's pavilion was actually discovered to be dead, although it did involve (stop the sniggering at the back) a member – the one that was the proud property of Michael Angelow. While, despite his name, he was a merchant navy cook rather than a great artist, he did paint a memorable picture when he burst on to the scene as the first cricket streaker, galloping to the middle in plimsoles only on the Friday of the Ashes Test, and hurdling the wickets at either end before disappearing into the arms of the law. (Because the stump cam had yet to be invented, viewers were spared the sight of a super-slo replay of his gymnastic display from an overly explicit angle). While Angelow was a pioneer in his field, he only did it for a bet, and (slightly furtive) research reveals no examples of him resorting to similar behaviour at subsequent sporting events. The same cannot be said of Bruce McAuley, the Kiwi lawnmower mechanic who, at Auckland a couple of years later, enjoyed his moment in the spotlight so much that he disrupted play with his naked cavortings on no fewer than three occasions. On his final sojourn to the wicket, this time clad in nothing but an enormous set of head-phones, Greg Chappell, the batsman, had seen enough and decided to take matters into his own hands, grasping hold of the miscreant and delivering six crossbat swipes to where the sun had rarely had a chance to shine. Unable to make a burst for freedom, McAuley could only timidly plead with the Australian not to hit him so hard.

Larrikin level

Medium. McAuley was still feeling a little sore when he appeared before magistrates the following day and was fined $75; a fellow streaker who should have been in court with him was probably a little ginger himself – his escape from a policeman who chased him the length of the field being completed only after he had extricated some particularly crucial personal belongings from the top of the barbed wire fence he had scaled.

Australia v England

1st Test. Perth. November 1982.

The intruder at Auckland in 1977 subsequently threatened to take Greg Chappell to court for assault, although police assured the Australian captain that he didn't have much of a case. Not that the Australian Cricket Board would have been particularly helpful in aiding Chappell build his defence. In fact, they would have been forced to admit that he had been acting with their implicit assent, a relevant sub-section of the board's code of conduct stating that although players, quite reasonably, "must not assault or attempt to assault an umpire, another player or a spectator" this did not apply "to any player's conduct towards any spectator trespassing on the ground". It is unlikely that Terry Alderman, the nigglingly accurate proponent of the arts of swing and seam who was to prove Graham Gooch's nemesis some years later, had the pertinent paragraphs to the forefront of his mind when he was cuffed on the back of the head by one of a number of uninvited English guests who took to the field draped in Union Jacks to celebrate their country's 400 on the second day of the first test at the WACA. Nevertheless, the infringement on his person drove him to pursue the offender, but his attempt to bring him to earth with an Australian Rules tackle was as badly timed as the connoisseurs of that sport in its hotbed of Melbourne might have expected from a Western Australian. When Alderman was eventually peeled off the outfield he was found to be suffering from a dislocated shoulder, which was to keep him out of the game for the remainder of the season.

Larrikin level

High. Lord Harris excepted, players have rarely been the main target of disenchanted spectators, so Alderman's shocked reaction could hardly be wholeheartedly condemned. At least Dennis Lillee and Allan Border completed Alderman's attempt at a citizen's arrest, but Greg Chappell had to lead his team from the ground for 14 minutes while order was fully restored. A total of 26 arrests were made.

9

India v Sri Lanka
World Cup semi-final. Calcutta. March 1996.

Effigies have had a hard time of it in Asia, regularly being strung up or burnt when things go wrong on the cricket field. It's a treatment that has been dished out to the likenesses of Wasim Akram and Mohammed Azharuddin among others, and there was no shortage of dummies for the India fans to get their teeth into when their side slumped from the promising position of 98 for two to 120 for eight as they chased a target of 252 to beat Sri Lanka and win a place in the World Cup final. Calcutta, the scene of this disaster, was no stranger to cricket chaos. As well as the previous example in 1967, there had

been trouble two years later, when Australia were the visitors. A stampede, as 20,000 people queued outside for the 8,000 cheap tickets available for the fourth day, resulted in the death of six of them. Later, as India slumped closer to a ten-wicket defeat, occupants in the higher tiers of some stands began dropping objects on to those below. As those on the receiving end sought safety on the outfield, one photographer, in his search for a picture, ventured too close to Bill Lawry, the Australia captain doing little to enhance his popularity by shoving the poor chap over. However, there is no doubt that the riot which will be most remembered was this one in 1996, a game which was serious box office, broadcast live to millions around the world. As India's challenge faded, the bottles began raining down on the outfield, and flames became visible in the stands as bundles of paper were set alight, forcing the players into a huddle in the middle. Clive Lloyd, the match referee, ordered them off after viewing the debris for himself, and though, after 20 minutes, the worst seemed to be over and the players resumed their positions, another bottle careened over the sightscreen, forcing Lloyd to abandon the match and award it to Sri Lanka.

Larrikin level

High. Unlike other riots in Calcutta, there could be no excuses or attempt to shift the blame. It was created by nothing more than the sulkiness of supporters as probable victory turned into certain defeat. What's more, it couldn't be blamed on India's underclasses; most of the 110,000 tickets had been distributed through official channels to the more privileged in the regional cricket associations. Sorry may indeed be the hardest word, but sadly it is not the pictures of some ashamed Indian fans later holding up placards proclaiming "Regret" and "Apologies" that are generally remembered.

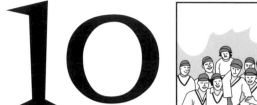

10

India v West Indies

Loyalty to the flag can be taken too far sometimes. Especially when the said flag is at the top of a pole on the roof of a pavilion, to which several thousand spectators angered by a ticket botch-up are trying to set light. Nevertheless, Barbadian Conrad Hunte, the effects of tear gas as well as patriotic emotion pouring from his eyes, was not to be put off, scaling the pole and saving the fluttering emblem of the Caribbean islands for the future. What kind of a future that was going to be was hard to imagine at that stage, as Hunte then joined several of his team-mates in clambering over the Eden Gardens perimeter fence and making a run for it. Several India players also fled on foot, while others were evacuated by car, a number of Bengal cricket officials and selectors secreted under the seats. What, you may ask, had brought about this sad state of affairs? The answer is, simply, incompetence. The demand for tickets to see the visiting unofficial world champions had been immense, and as the crowd surged in for the start of the second day, many were bemused to find their seats already occupied by a spectator whose ticket bore the same number as theirs. As rumours spread about a forgery scandal, hundreds of fans were forced on to the grass beyond the boundary, where they were confronted by police, who added to the fun by lathi-charging them and hurling tear-gas grenades into the stand. Furious hand to hand combat ensued, while other enraged spectators carried benches to the middle for an impromptu bonfire and gouged holes in the pitch with stumps.

Larrikin level

Medium. A subsequent inquiry blamed mismanagement by the Bengal Cricket Association, which led to overcrowding at the 57,000-capacity stadium, and serious over-reaction by the police. Play resumed the following day only after the teams had been promised danger bonus payments and against a background of charred stands and gaps where the benches had been. But one man was happy. Lance Gibbs, the West Indies spinner, found purchase on the damaged pitch to pick up match figures of seven for 88 as India collapsed to an innings defeat.

117

11  India v Australia

1st Test. Bombay. November 1969.

In an era when Johnners, Blowers and the like were still waxing lyrical about their view of London buses as they passed by The Oval (between gulping down mouthfuls of Black Forest Gateau provided by a member of their audience), Indian commentators were getting stuck into a portion of something less agreeable: controversy. Perhaps now, looking back on the fateful fourth day of this Test in the coastal city, Devraj Puri would wish he had restricted his comments to an appreciation of listeners' culinary generosity. Instead, his condemnation of umpire Sambhu Pan's decision to give Srinivasaraghavan

Venkataraghavan out caught behind gave local spectators, facing the defeat of their heroes, something to get their teeth into when it was simultaneously transmitted to hundreds of radios in the East Stand. Possibly possessing a sixth sense about the potential for trouble in Puri's opinion, co-commentator Madhav Mantri tried to step into the breach, suggesting expressing a viewpoint "from this far out" was not altogether wise. But it was too late, the damage was done, or it was about to be. As bottles and stones were hurled on to the outfield, a section of the crowd marched out and set fire to the tennis courts at the back of the stand. Others set alight parts of the North and Bombay Cricket Association Stands before standing back to admire their contribution as a breeze coming off the sea fanned the flames and sent smoke billowing across the playing area. As the game continued despite it all, Jehangir Irani, an elderly scorer, went on to the pitch to complain that he couldn't see the umpire's signals, while a reporter from the *Indian Express*, GK Menon, ran out to demand play be suspended. He got short shrift from Bill Lawry, the Australian captain, who felt the whole incident was a ploy by spectators to help India save the match.

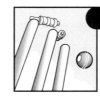

Larrikin level

High. The Australians had to wait behind on the pitch for 20 minutes after the close as riot police cleared refugees from the burning stands from in front of the club-house sightscreen. Even as they finally trooped off – one or two holding stumps for protection – John Gleeson was knocked to the ground by a flying bottle. When they finally reached the supposed safety of the pavilion, Lawry had a wicker chair dropped on him from a balcony above. However, the greatest casualty was the reputation of the Bombay crowd, which had no history of such behaviour.

119

12  Twelfth Man
(and, in this case, animal)

The occupants of Headingley's Western Terrace, while single-handedly keeping the purveyors of fancy dress finery in business, have rarely been lauded for their diplomacy, the propulsion of a pig's head wrapped in a plastic bag into an enclosure of Pakistan supporters during the 1992 Test match providing a perfect example of the level of their cultural sensitivity. Over the years, the authorities have pulled their hair out in the search for a solution, even going so far as to impose a blanket ban on alcohol in the area to quell the redneck rowdiness of its residents. Finally, in 1997, acting on the premise that you get the stewards you deserve, they imported a bunch of rugby league forwards to help police the section. This was bad news for the few true humorists in the crowd who, rather than simply dressing as women then shouting ribald abuse whenever a real representative of the sex walked by, had taken some degree of care in their choice of outfit. Brancha Resic, for example, had opted for a sweaty day not only as the butt of unfunny jokes, but as a butt *per se* – the back end of a pantomime cow. After a day of changeable weather conditions which made him unsure whether to remain in his seat or stand up, he linked up with his front end and set out for an evening graze on the Headingley outfield. For the stewards it was like a red rag to a bull, five of them stampeding in as if the synthetic bovine was about to cross in the corner for the winning try in the Tetley's Super League play-off final. Despite frantic calls from onlookers of "they're behind you", poor Brancha was oblivious to the danger, taking the full force of the tackle and being crunched into the boundary boards. Half an hour later, after oxygen had been administered, he regained consciousness, but had to be carted off to Leeds General for treatment to a serious neck injury.

Chapter Six

The
Worst
Upsets

123

The Worst Upsets

t is a cruel fact of cricket that one man's success is another's failure. Kipling would, of course, have addressed this dichotomy by burbling on about meeting triumph and disaster and treating the two imposters just the same, but then he never played the game – and, besides, you get an awful lot of disaster to go with your, frankly, limited triumphs (unless you're an Australian Test player of a recent generation). And, even if you are, as a rule, fairly successful, that only lines you up for the mother of all falls, what is usually described as an upset, or a shock. But the word upset doesn't just imply the victory of a David over a Goliath; it can also refer to a state of mind, situations that cause outrage or pain, or, as shall be seen, incidents altogether more messy...

1

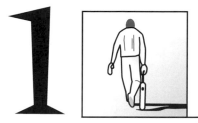

England's Lesson
Australian Academy v England
One-day games. North Sydney Oval.
December 1994.

More like Australian Academy versus the Police Academy. After losing a day to rain, England plumbed new depths of inadequacy after requesting the scheduled three-day game be replaced by two limited-overs matches to give them some practice for the forthcoming triangular tournament. Bad move. In the Saturday encounter, Mike Gatting was dismissed first ball for a duck, as the Aussies overhauled their target by five wickets with ten balls to spare; in the Sunday sequel, the students got really personal, running out opener Alec Stewart before he had faced a ball and passing England's total with 41 balls unused, Daniel Marsh, the son of the former Australian wicketkeeper Rod, showing he had been well taught by hitting the winning runs.

Fallout Rating

3/10

If England had had their own academy at the time, Ofsted would have closed it down on account of bad results. When England, almost a decade later, did come round to the sense of establishing their own seat of cricket learning, it was Rod Marsh, who had headed the Australian version for a number of years, that they turned to.

2

World Cup Shock
Kenya v West Indies
Group match. Pune. February 1996.

One reaction to this result, a resounding 73-run win for the minnows which was likened to a pub team beating Manchester United, might be regarded as providing a significant insight into its cause. While the former West Indies greats, Michael Holding and Colin Croft, were united in their grief, mourning the loss of a proud tradition of success they had bequeathed their ungrateful successors and wailing and gnashing their teeth at the depths to which their beloved country had sunk, Richie Richardson, who presided over the debacle, was taking a more relaxed approach: "It's not the end of the world," said the personable Antiguan, showing an almost appealing inability to grasp the reality of a situation equalled only by his clueless attempts to motivate his sulky charges. In fact, it wasn't even the end of the West Indies' World Cup, a Lara-inspired victory over South Africa carrying them as far as the semi-finals, but apart from the unrest in the Caribbean camp, the Kenyan triumph was founded on what was generally agreed to be their weaker suit, their bowling. Batting first, their relatively highly-rated line-up had struggled to 88 for six, until Maurice Odumbe, the captain, was able to call on that experienced native of many an international match, extras, who nudged and nurdled their way to a top score of 35 (being particularly severe on anything wide or no-balled) and boosting the total to 166. When the West Indies replied, the underdogs embarked on a dastardly plan to bowl straight, allowing the batsmen, who appeared to regard time in the middle as an inconvenient barrier to carrying on a dispute with a team-mate in the dressing-room, to cut short their contributions and thus post a World Cup low of 93.

Fallout Rating

7/10

Three big cheers for the Kenyan players, who even surprised themselves with their victory, and a few tears for Richardson, who fell on his sword at the end of the tournament before the West Indies Cricket Board could run it through him. Odumbe, who revered his opponents, counting Brian Lara as one of his biggest idols, memorably declared: "Before the match all I wanted to get was his autograph, but I ended up with his wicket."

3 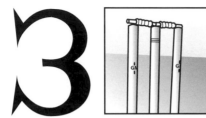 Don Bradman's Swansong
England v Australia
5th Test. The Oval. August 1948.

After years of trying, England finally discovered a foolproof way, far removed from the excesses of Bodyline, to remove the little Aussie genius: make him cry. Unfortunately, it was a bit too late to reverse the balance of power in Ashes contests – it was Bradman's last innings for his country. Coming to the wicket needing just four runs to ensure a Test average of 100, the Don was so overcome with emotion when the fielders gathered round, gave him three cheers and wished him luck that he was temporarily reduced to a blubbering mortal who could only whimper softly as he poked at Eric Hollies' apparent leg-break, and watched a perfect googly pirouette almost apologetically through his defective defence and dislodge his off bail.

Fallout Rating

5/10

Cricket's delightful propensity for irony was obviously at work here, setting the stage for a command performance only to rip open the trap-door and deny the Don the opportunity of a triumphant curtain call. You can be sure there was barely a dry eye in the house as the duck condemned the great man to a career Test average of 99.94, which no other performer has got within 40 runs of since. Despite the great entertainer's negligible contribution with the bat, Australia still recorded an innings victory after scoring 389, completing a 4-0 series win. England, who hadn't won an Ashes series since Bodyline in 1932-33, had to wait until the fifth Test of the 1953 home series to recapture the little urn.

Zimbabwe's First Test Victory
Zimbabwe v Pakistan
1st Test. Harare. January/February 1995.

Disputed tosses, throwing bowlers, bribery allegations – and umpires accused of ball-tampering: a month was a long time in Zimbabwe cricket. Pakistan arrived in Harare on the back of a series victory over Australia and three one-day wins in South Africa. Good reason, you might think, to be confident against Test cricket's weakest link, still looking for a first triumph after 11 matches. But the visitors might have realised it was going to be one of those games when Jackie Hendricks, the match referee, ordered the toss to be carried out a second time because Salim Malik had called "bird", the national symbol on the Zimbabwean coin, instead of the orthodox "heads". Andy Flower won the re-flick, chose to bat and proceeded to star in a third-wicket partnership of 269 with his brother Grant. Pakistan never recovered and slumped to an ignominious innings defeat in four days.

Fallout Rating

12/10

The repercussions were amazing. Malik accused home umpire Ian Robinson of rubbing sweat on one side of the ball in the third Test, and allegations of Pakistani match-fixing attempts spiralled, forcing the tourists to swear on the Koran that they were innocent. In the subsequent one-day series, Bryan Strang was fined for pointing an opposition batsman to the pavilion, but this was waived when he protested he was only showing him the way to the Ladbrokes tent.

Sri Lanka's World Cup Triumph

Sri Lanka v Australia

Final. Lahore. March 1996.

England stuttered miserably around Asia, the West Indians quarrelled, the Pakistanis and Indians had their effigies burned, and the Australians fretted about the safety of going shopping in a Colombo recently bombed in the ongoing civil strife: an uncharitable historian might assume the Sri Lankans, shorn of two of their four home matches because of that internal friction, sneaked to the title by default, a mixture of luck and sub-continental cunning. But they didn't. They upheld Asian honour by blasting their way through to the final and an ultimate victory over the world's best team, each Jayasuriya boundary emphasising the innovative approach which turned the accepted wisdom of one-day cricket on its head and reverberating with the number of syllables in his name. Captain Arjuna Ranatunga also chose to contravene the prevailing philosophy on World Cup finals, putting the Australians in after winning the toss, even though no team batting second had hitherto won the title. If it was a tactic based on reverse psychology it seemed to have failed utterly as the favourites cantered to 134 for one in 25 overs. But once Mark Taylor was caught on the boundary, Ranatunga used his quartet of spinners to strangle the innings to such an extent that only one boundary was scored in the second 25. The loss of two early wickets failed to suppress Sri Lankan confidence, as Aravinda de Silva guided his side to a seven wicket win under the lights with 22 deliveries remaining.

Fallout Rating

9/10

Set the cat amongst the pigeons. Shane Warne had to be consoled by coach Bobby Simpson after recording his third worst one-day figures, while Sri Lanka's determination to hit over the top when the new fielding restrictions were in force for the opening 15 overs leant the misappropriated term of pinch-hitter to the game's vocabulary and created a fresh template for one-day cricket the world over. But a country granted Test status in 1981 still had to wait until 2002 before getting a full three-match series in England.

6

The Miracle of Leeds
England v Australia
3rd Test. Headingley. July 1981.

England had slumped to 135-7 in their second innings, still 92 adrift of Australia in the follow-on, when Ian Botham, relieved of the pressures of captaincy by the recall of Mike Brearley following his pair at Lord's, met Graham Dilley for a mid-pitch conference. Foregoing the usual extension of pleasantries, the encouragement to play for tea or the coaxing of a tailender who had scored only 11 runs in seven innings against the West Indies the previous winter to "just get in line", Botham summoned up five words, simple in expression, but devastating in impact. "Let's give it some humpty," the country's greatest all-rounder told his partner,

an appropriate assertion given that at that stage, it looked as if not even all the king's horses and all the king's men could have put England back together again. In the event, it was the Aussies who suffered a great fall, the home side smashing 216 in the next 35 overs as Botham wielded a bat borrowed from Graham Gooch to much greater effect than its owner (who'd scored 2 and 0), while Dilley, Chris Old and Bob Willis got stuck in at the other end. By the time the innings was over, with Beefy undefeated on 149, Australia needed 130 to win, which shouldn't have been beyond them, especially when they advanced to 56 for one. But they hadn't reckoned on Willis, the 6'5" paceman with the mass of fuzzy hair who'd been stung on his first visit to Australia in 1970 to be told by a home spectator that he "didn't know they stacked crap that high". Now, he was like a man possessed by the memory of that insult, hurtling down the hill from the Kirkstall Lane end, his bounce and lift capturing eight of the next nine wickets for the addition of only 55 runs as England snatched the unlikeliest of victories by 18 runs.

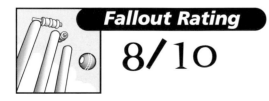

Fallout Rating

8/10

The turnaround was remarkable. England, trailing 1-0 in the six match series, and without a Test win in 12 games, had been so certain of defeat by the end of the third day that the players went to Botham's house to drown their sorrows, many of them, Willis included, convinced that their international careers were about to end. As it was, most retained their places for the remainder of the season, as England went on to win 3-1. The only bleak spot was that viewers in Australia were saved from witnessing the catastrophe, as ABC technicians pulled the plug at the start of each day's play in a wages dispute.

7 The George Davis Affair
England v Australia
3rd Test. Headingley. August 1975.

Digging up a Test match track on the eve of the fifth day of a delicately-poised Ashes encounter to get publicity for your cause may be acceptable if you've suffered a miscarriage of justice on the scale of the Guildford Four. Arguably. But the major flaw in the George Davis is Innocent campaign was that he wasn't, was he? Three years after campaign leader Peter Chappell squeezed under the Headingley covers at midnight armed with a knife, fork and oil to have dinner for one by torchlight, Davis, a 34-year-old minicab driver, was back inside, a 15-year sentence the result of his involvement in an armed bank raid. And, as a man drawn to crime as inexorably as Mike Gatting was to offering his front pad to balls cutting back from outside the off stump, Davis had only been free for a matter of months when, in July 1987, he was convicted again, this time of trying to rob a mail train.

Fallout Rating
6/10

Seriously upsetting for England. The Aussies still needed 225 to win with seven wickets in hand, but this was a four-match series and they were already 1-0 up and in possession of the Ashes. No wonder captain Ian Chappell – no relation to the campaign leader (honest, guv) – was seriously reluctant to continue the match on an adjoining strip.

8

Alas Smith and Jones

India v Australia 1st Test. Madras. September 1986.

England v UAE World Cup group match.

Peshawar. February 1996.

Although separated by almost a decade, the Victoria and Australia batsman Dean Jones and the Warwickshire and England player Neil Smith took part in two of the greatest upsets on a cricket field. Stomach upsets, that is. Jones spent the day retching, aptly enough by the return crease, as he defied a severe dose of Madras belly to compile 210. Yet it was so nearly in vain: by the time Ray Bright had Maninder Singh leg-before to complete only the second tied Test, Jones was connected to an intra-venous drip. Smith, an offspinner, took his skipper's instructions to throw it up a little too literally. Okay, in truth he was batting by the time he decided to regurgitate his refuelling requirements in front of a worldwide TV audience of millions.

Fallout Rating

10/10

Plenty, mostly all over the bowlers' follow-throughs. At least Smith had the decency to wait until the sixteenth over and the removal of the close fielders. Nevertheless, the sickly pair knew how to spill their guts for your country, even if their behaviour would have been instantly recognisable to the average Birmingham Balti House waiter at closing time.

9

Holland's Giant-Killing
The Netherlands v Australia
One-innings match. The Hague. 1964.

When, in the most recent World Cup in South Africa, Australia lined up against Holland, a team of amateurs who had had to qualify from the preliminary tournament months earlier, the bookmakers were taking no chances: so favoured were the Australians, almost invincible in one-day cricket, that odds of 2000-1 on were imposed on a victory by Ricky Ponting's side. This despite the latter of only two previous contests between the two sides, 39 years earlier, resulting in an incredible boost for Dutch courage at a time when the Australians, fresh from an Ashes series victory in England, were powerful, if not quite as dominant. The Australians may point to mitigating circumstances: the presence of a matting wicket, which forced the players to wear

138

plimsoles instead of spikes, and the zest of their hosts to show them the delights of local coffee shops on the eve of the match, but the parking lot of Vans (Van der Vergt, van Arkel and van Weelde) proved too strong for their illustrious visitors, grinding out a three-wicket victory in front of a 4,000-strong crowd.

Fallout Rating

4/10

Embarrassing, but hardly terminal. Although it was almost so for

one Australian player, Jack Potter. The Victorian, who had failed to get a Test under his belt in England, was hit on the head, the absence of protection in this helmetless era resulting in a fractured skull which was sufficient to scupper his chances of getting a Test cap when the team stopped off in India on the way home. He never got an opportunity again, although much later, as the first head of the Australian Academy in Adelaide, he taught Shane Warne the flipper.

10

Bumble's Outburst
Zimbabwe v England
1st Test. Bulawayo. December 1996.

Sadly, the phrase "we flippin' murdered 'em" was not an admission of guilt by upholders of the repugnant Robert Mugabe regime on the fate of political opponents. It was coined by David Lloyd, the England coach on this tour to southern Africa, who was very upset indeed by his team's inability to win the inaugural Test between the two countries in Bulawayo, the only one in history to have finished drawn with the scores level. To be fair, there was some "previous" involving the two sides. In 1992, the chicken farmer Eddo Brandes had dismissed the Zimbabwean-turned-Englishman Graeme Hick for a duck while inspiring his team,

at that time still only an associate member of the ICC, to a stunning nine-run World Cup victory over the country that invented the game. Later that year, when Zimbabwe were allowed into the Test club, England sniffily abstained from the vote. Lloyd's ire was aimed at Zimbabwean tactics, which saw them bowl increasingly wide of leg and off stumps without censure, as the tourists chased 205 in 37 overs on the final day. Stewart and Knight had inspired England to 107 for one by the halfway stage at tea, but the loss of crucial wickets left them needing 13 off the final over. When Knight smacked Heath Streak for six off the first ball, Lloyd must have thought his team were home and dry, but Streak sneaked in another unpunished wide one that left the England opener looking for three off the last ball. He looked to have smacked a winning boundary, but Stuart Carlisle's incredible stop was returned rapidly and Knight was run out looking for the third.

Fallout Rating

7/10

Lloyd, now plying his opinions on Sky TV, is affectionately known as Bumble, apparently because of his enthusiastic verbosity imparted with an incomprehensible Lancashire buzz. But his outpourings here got him labelled as something more of a bumbling idiot when he added to his not inconsiderable oral crimes with the bleedingly obvious comment "one more ball and we'd have walked it". He was roundly mocked for failing to take into account the fact that England had batted inexplicably slowly in their first innings, and had allowed Zimbabwe's last four second-innings wickets to add 127 while occupying 56 overs.

11

Pluck of the Irish
Ireland v West Indies
Two innings one-day match. Sion Mills. July 1969.

Whether it was because they had been confused by consumption of too much of the black stuff, or the clever Irish ruse of insisting on a two innings match in one day (with the winner being declared on first-innings score in the result of the second innings being incomplete) it is hard to know, but the West Indies, containing six of the players who would start the third Test against England later that month, slumped to 25 all out, the Irish captain Goodwin claiming five for six and Clyde Walcott, the team manager, showing the rest how to do it with a top score of nine. Ireland responded with 125 for eight declared, allowing West Indies to reach 78 for four at the second time of asking before stumps were pulled. Counting back, Ireland were awarded that match by nine wickets, having passed the tourists' first innings score with only one wicket down.

Fallout Rating
4/10

The West Indies took it out on the Welsh instead, Basil Butcher smashing 151 and Clive Lloyd a double century at Swansea on their return from across the Irish sea.

12

Twelfth Man (or in this case Woman)

Bradman XI v World XI

Charity match. Sydney. December 1994.

Zoe Goss was an all-round sporting Sheila, partial to a bit of softball, netball, and basketball, who only discovered cricket in her teens when she began to mix it with the boys at Perth Modern Senior High. Brian Lara was the world's greatest batsman, with a record Test score of 375 to his name. But when their paths crossed at the SCG, Goss, the only female member of the Bradman XI, triumphed. Bowling to the World XI's biggest star, she got him out. Twice. In one delivery. First, she drew him forward and tempted him into edging her to wicketkeeper Steve Rixon who, taking no chances, whipped off the bails as the humbled genius over-balanced. It was no fluke, either. She went on to dismiss Jeff Dujon as well.

Chapter Seven

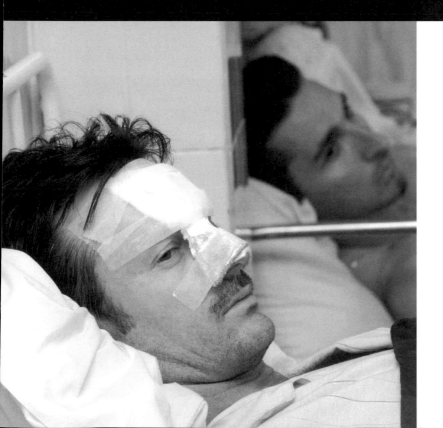

Worst

Injuries

143

Worst Injuries

Cricket at the highest levels has been likened to war minus the shooting. And in war it is common for blood to be spilt – a little in heroic sacrifice or tragically self-inflicted, some through the simple misfortune of being in the wrong place at the wrong time, but mostly because of the bastard on the other side who's out to get you (or out to get you out). Such bastards can use a variety of tactics, from the brutal attempt to force outright surrender to the more subtle approach in which the enemy is undermined by fear and intimidation. Mike Denness, the England captain whose side was pummelled into submission by that inimitable chin music hall act Lillee and Thomson in Australia in 1974–75, observed in an account of the tour that the cynical excesses of short-pitched bowling could encourage spectators to attend purely in expectation of seeing a bit of the red stuff. *"I don't think fans want to see lots of people being hit on the head or getting broken ribs,"* he said.

Oh no? He might have been right: but despite our better natures, viewing figures for the 24–hour news channels during the Iraq War confirm that this sort of thing can provide addictive entertainment and the boos of at least some members of the crowd must be taken as little more than pantomime derision.

1

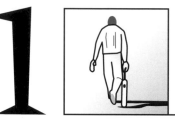

A.C.M. Croome

Lancashire v Gloucestershire

County Championship. Old Trafford. June 1887.

Alexander Croome is a man sometimes credited with creating the technique for modern hurdlers during his time at Oxford University. Britain's showing at a century of Olympic Games since may owe something to the fact that it had its flaws. That, at least, would appear to be the case if Croome's effort to clear the railings surrounding the Old Trafford playing area as he ran out of room trying to cut off a boundary during this game was typical. Instead of leaping comfortably over them and charging up the pavilion steps to take the tape, he succeeded only in impaling himself on them. By the throat. There he might have remained hanging, a gruesome monument to the truism that no bowler's figures are worth that degree of sacrifice, but for the grace of, well, Dr WG, his legendary medically-qualified Gloucestershire team-mate. The bearded one, more renowned for holding together his team's innings than the gaping neck of an injured co-worker, was forced to keep the wound plugged with his bare hands until, half an hour later, a surgical needle and thread was located and the hapless Croome was stitched up and hastened to hospital.

A&E waiting time

Under-staffing being what it was, even in those pre-NHS days, WG Grace was committed to care in the community. When, some years later, UM Fox, of Kent, dislocated his shoulder in a match against Gloucestershire, WG enjoined fellow physician and elder brother, EM Grace, to sit on the fielder's head while he, with one foot embedded against Fox's body, yanked the offending part back into place.

Mike Gatting
West Indies v England
One-day international. Jamaica. February 1986.

It's a little known fact that during this limited overs match which followed the first Test at Sabina Park, Malcolm Marshall, the feared West Indies fast bowler, was halted in mid run-up by an umpire who suspected him of applying an illegal substance to the ball; an international incident was only averted when forensic analysis showed the said material to be part of Mike Gatting's nose. The Middlesex captain had earlier taken leave of proceedings clutching at the remnants of his proboscis, mostly projected inwards, after a Marshall bouncer had caused a creative rearrangement of his facial features. After a few minutes recovering in the dressing room, the ever-competitive batsman was ready to resumethe fight with the West Indian pace battalion until some brave soul steeled himself to point out to him that the ball had gone directly from his face on to his stumps.

A&E waiting time

Airlifted to England for treatment, Gatting recuperated on a visual diet of his beloved Dr Who videos – not entirely apt since his bruised and bloodied head had swollen up like something that would have unnerved John Merrick let alone Jon Pertwee. After an absence of 23 days, he was back in the Caribbean, only, on his return to action against Barbados, to have his thumb broken by Vibert Greene. The injury kept him out of the fourth Test at Bridgetown and may have made him wish he could use his favourite timelord's mode of transport to turn back the clock and start the series again.

Andy Lloyd
England v West Indies
1st Test. Edgbaston. June 1984.

It's every boy's dream come true. You're opening the batting in your first Test match. Remembering the words of wisdom of countless coaches and commentators, you set yourself little targets, breathing a silent sigh of relief as each is reached. You turn the ball behind square for a single to get off the mark, craft a clip through mid-wicket for your first boundary; a firm push to the weaker hand of mid-off brings up double figures. Then, from out of the blue, the bowler conjures up a delivery of such unexpected ferocity that the ball spears from his hand as an incomprehensible blur; your eyes record it, but your consciousness fails to register the seriousness of the situation. In a split-second, your peace of mind, as well as pieces of your fibre-glass helmet, are shattered. You are on the ground, lying motionless, your concerned opponents gradually looming in and out of focus above you. Recovering from the initial shock, you are led groggily from the field to sympathetic applause from the first-morning crowd. You spend eight days in hospital with blurred vision. You are never called on by your country again.

 ## A&E waiting time

Bed freed up immediately for Andy Lloyd, the unfortunate Warwickshire

left-hander who lived this story to the letter but who refused to blame Malcolm Marshall, once again the bowler who delivered the fateful ball. "Cricket's a hard game. The ball's hard. It hurts," Lloyd said with unparalleled understatement as he sat out eight months in the recovery position. Just how hard, he was about to find out: as he sought to return to full fitness during pre-season training, he strained his back; a few weeks later, he suffered whiplash in a car crash; and within the month, he was sidelined again after Richard Hadlee dislocated his finger. Lesser mortals would have taken the hint, but Lloyd battled on gamely for another seven seasons.

4

Wan Chatfield
New Zealand v England
1st Test. Auckland. February 1975.

There's much talk these days – and we hope it is largely metaphorical – about players being prepared to die for their country. Ewan Chatfield is probably the only one who did. The No 11, stubbornly resisting the England bowlers who needed only his wicket or that of partner Geoff Howarth to wrap up victory on the fifth morning, was struck on the temple by a rearing delivery from Peter Lever, collapsed, swallowed his tongue and started to turn blue. While the England physiotherapist Bernard Thomas – immediately recognizing the gravity of his plight – raced on, administered heart massage to the stricken Test debutant, whose ticker had temporarily given up the ghost, and carried out mouth-to-mouth resuscitation, Lever, sabotaging any hopes he harboured for a future career as a paramedic, sat on the stumps and sobbed. Still, it was one way to win a Test.

A&E waiting time

Straight into surgery for Chatfield, who finally recovered consciousness after some intensive care. It was another harsh introduction to international cricket but, unlike Andy Lloyd, the Wellington bowler went on to become a crucial figure in New Zealand cricket as the foil to Richard Hadlee's rapier-like thrusts. He even earned an MBE for his services to the game, thankfully not posthumously.

David Lawrence
New Zealand v England
3rd Test. Wellington. February 1992.

Chatfield may have risen from the dead to enjoy a moderately successful career but for David Lawrence, nicknamed Syd after the well-known band leader who shared his surname, New Zealand was the place the music died. The big-hearted Gloucestershire paceman, whose approach to the wicket was once likened to a rampaging elephant with its tail on fire, was, as ever, giving his all despite a game that was petering out to an inevitable draw. But as he wound up into his delivery stride one more time, the batsman was left with his bat waving irrelevantly in the air as a noise like a gunshot rang out around the Basin Reserve. Lawrence crumpled to the ground screaming in agony as if he'd been snared by a desperately inept ivory poacher. What had actually happened was that his studs had caught in the footholes on landing, snapping his kneecap clean in two.

A&E waiting time

Eventually stretchered off, it might have been kinder for any available marksman to have put the writhing Lawrence out of his misery. For two years this genuinely fast bowler, who had broken Trevor Franklin's arm early in the tour, battled to regain sufficient fitness to return to the game, but had to admit defeat when the kneecap went again.

6

The Indians
West Indies v India
4th Test, Jamaica, April 1976.

I t is a cricketing mantra that you have to take 20 wickets to win a Test match. This game, on a typically bouncy surface at Sabina Park, was the exception that proves the rule: Clive Lloyd's men needed just 11. Lloyd, disillusioned by the pace pummelling his side had taken at the hands of Australia in the winter – and the ineffectiveness of the new spinners selected for the previous three Tests in place of the 41-year-old Lance Gibbs – opted for a four-pronged attack of speed merchants, headed by a rampant Michael Holding who was ordered to use the opposition batsmen – á la Bodyline – for target practice from round the wicket. Anshuman Gaekwad, a bespectacled opener, became the first Indian to suffer, brought to his knees by a smack on the temple; Gundappa Viswanath, the second, with a broken finger. By the time a rapidly-revolving seam had kissed Brijesh Patel impertinently full on the lips, Bishen Bedi had seen enough. Ordering his remaining troops to retreat to the safety of the dressing-room, the India skipper raised the white flag by declaring with only six wickets down as he sought to keep his own spinning fingers and those of Bhagwat Chandrasekhar out of harm's way. His submissive approach failed to have the desired effect: Bedi injured his bowling hand anyway as he tried to take a return catch from Viv Richards and Chandrasekhar was forced to the dressing-room when his arm took the full force of a West Indian attacking

A&E waiting time

With five players forced to join the queue for treatment at the Kingston General, there were not too many stomachs available for the fight and the Indian second innings ended on an incomplete 97 for five, leaving the home side requiring just 13 for victory. At least Surinder Armanath, one of six substitute fielders called on by the tourists, provided the senior house officer with a different challenge: he was wheeled in to the operating theatre with a burst appendix.

7

Rick McCosker
Australia v England
Centenary Test. Melbourne. 1977.

If there's one thing likely to irritate the cricketers of any contemporary generation, it is the carping from the sidelines of former greats whose deeds were carried out in an era when only two forms of the game existed; long and longer. The likes of Fred Trueman or Trevor Bailey rarely had to throw themselves around in the field or adopt the slide position to haul back a possible boundary. Neither, to be fair, did Greg Chappell, the Australia captain for this celebratory occasion, although the influence of one-day cricket on the three, four and five-day games was beginning to filter into cricket's collective consciousness (and would be given further impetus as Kerry Packer chose this year to raise his not particularly attractive head). Nevertheless, the demands on players were growing, so it was no surprise that Chappell should experience a fit of pique when a vocal number of the 218 former cricketers who turned up to mark their part in 100 years of Ashes Tests promptly started moaning about the quality of entertainment on offer. However, even the most reactionary among them – and there were Bodyline survivors present – would have found it hard to find anything but words of praise for Rick McCosker as events unfolded. The opening batsman had had his jaw broken by Bob Willis in the first innings, but the man nicknamed "The General" was determined to take the battle to the enemy even though his swollen head was swathed in bandages like something from *The Mummy Returns*,

by the time he surprised team-mates and spectators by appearing at No. 10 in Australia's second innings. Once there, he helped Rod Marsh to his century in a crucial ninth-wicket partnership that would ultimately decide the match in his side's favour.

A&E waiting time

Willis could not forgive himself afterwards for not trying to send his opponent straight back to the emergency room. "I went a bit soft on McCosker. I should have bounced the poop out of him when he came back," he moaned. "But I suppose that's why we're English and they're Australian."

8

Jason Gillespie and Steve Waugh
Sri Lanka v Australia
1st Test. Kandy. September 1999.

Steve Waugh has eked out a profitable little sideline in tour diaries, though one can't help thinking that they generally can't make for particularly varied reading: July 1993: retained Ashes; February 1995: beat England again; July 1997: beat the Poms; February 1999: stuffed the bloody Mother Country; November 2002: stuffed the bloody Poms again (with two Tests to spare). Etc. etc. Nevertheless, persevere, and you will find the entry for September 10, 1999, somewhat more entertaining. Well, actually there is no entry for that date, the Australian captain having so disfigured himself in a horrifying collision with Jason Gillespie (nicknamed Dizzy, and no doubt he was after the two met head-on pursuing a catch around the back of square leg) that he had to wait for two days until the swelling on his nose had subsided before being able to submit his thoughts to paper again. (Even then he still resembled a cross between Pinnochio and the child-catcher from *Chitty Chitty Bang Bang*.) Waugh reported that he had been running back from his position just behind square when he had lost sight of the ball in the sun and elected to dive headlong in a vain attempt to pouch it; Gillespie, loping in off the boundary, was equally committed to the cause but from the ensuing entanglement of bodies and limbs, emerged not with the ball but a broken leg.

A&E waiting time

The pair were packed into a van for the journey to a local hospital, but it wasn't the end of their troubles as many of the occupants of a packed emergency ward shuffled and limped towards them in the hope of getting their autographs. Packed off finally to Colombo by helicopter for surgery, indignity was added to Gillespie's agony as the suppositories being applied to relieve his pain twice failed to hit their intended target and his smirking skipper, pen in hand, was there to record the chastening moment.

9

Kevin Badcock

Queensland v Tasmania

Gillette Cup. Brisbane. December 1976.

Bowlers, especially of the fast or medium-fast variety, are the great martyrs of the game, convinced that they are the unappreciated servants of a sport in which batsmen are king. Wherever you go in the cricketing world you will be obliged to listen to their almost endless list of gripes and grievances: being forced to operate from the wrong end, often uphill and into the wind; being compelled to perform on a pitch as unresponsive as a monk at a swingers' convention; how the footholes are too firm, or too giving; how there is too little swing, or too much; the futility of hoping for a leg-before decision on the front foot. All these complainants, however, forget one particularly salient thing: they have the ball, which they can use to injure the batsman, both literally and (dis)figuratively. While the records are full of bowlers inflicting all manner of damage on their opponents, it is extraordinarily rare to come across examples of the opposite. Rare, but not unheard of. Kevin Badcock, a Tasmanian off-spinner, was one of the few unfortunates, taking a full-blooded drive from Viv Richards, then playing for Queensland, right on the face and suffering a depressed cheekbone during this 40-over a side Australian domestic competition. Helmets for bowlers, anyone?

A&E waiting time

Badcock was left to overnight at the Princess Alexandra Hospital in Brisbane as his team-mates flew back to Hobart. It was ironic really. The team, which had yet to be admitted to the Sheffield Shield, had prepared for the match, and suspected thunderbolts from Jeff Thomson, by facing a bowling machine sending down 90mph deliveries on a specially quickened matting surface. In the event, Thomson was ineffective and it was Greg Chappell's dibbly-dobbly off-cutters that reduced the visitors from 77 for four to 89 all out.

10

Anil Kumble
West Indies v India
4th Test. Antigua. May 2002.

Any bowler sending a batsman back to the pavilion with a broken jaw is entitled to think that that is the last his team will see of him or at least a couple of Tests. It was something no doubt that would have occurred to Mervyn Dillon, the West Indies paceman whose rising delivery thumped Anil Kumble on the chin and created such reverberations inside his mouth that a number of his teeth were left hanging precariously from his top gum. But Kumble was made of sterner stuff. For one, he didn't immediately recognize that his jaw was fractured, although his inability to contribute much to end-of-the-over meetings with his fellow batsman might have offered a clue, and he continued to fend off the dangerous Dillon until he was snapped up at short leg a few overs later. The following morning, a visit to a local hospital confirmed the gravity of the situation, he was put on a liquid diet and told to prepare to return to his homeland for surgery. However, Kumble, perhaps mindful of his exclusion from the first two Tests of the series and of a St John's pitch that was beginning to turn enough to keep a wrist spinner interested, determined to play on, metaphorically setting his jaw as the Antiguan medical authorities covered him from crown to Adam's Apple with dressings to keep him from literally losing face in the jarring of his delivery stride. Perhaps alarmed by the apparition approaching him from the opposite end, Brian Lara succumbed for a meagre four, lbw to the Indian, who returned the highly creditable figures of one for 29 from his 14 overs.

 A&E waiting time

The injection of adrenaline prevented Kumble from suffering too much discomfort while he remained in action, but it was a different matter when he came off the pitch, and he was dispatched to Bangalore for an operation, missing the final Test.

11

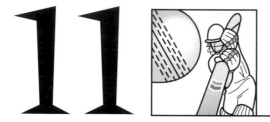

Fred Morley
Somewhere in the Indian Ocean
1882

Whatever misfortunes befall you in life, there is bound to be some smart-arse just waiting for the opportunity to remind you that "worse things happen at sea". In fact this is quite often true. Take the case of Fred Morley, the Nottinghamshire and England left-armer who returned the best analysis of eight for 146 in the Test against Australia at The Oval in 1880. Two years later, on his first ocean voyage to the Antipodes as part of the Hon. Ivo Bligh's England team, he was to discover that pitching and tossing were not expressions restricted to cricket terminology, the wayward vessel on which he was travelling ploughing into another during a storm as they rounded Sri Lanka (or Ceylon as it was in those Imperial days), landing him with a set of broken ribs.

A&E waiting time

Patched up in the ship's sick bay, Morley bravely battled on, playing four Tests down under. But his health deteriorated rapidly once he had returned home, consumption and dropsy bringing a premature end to his playing career – and his life – at the age of 34. Poignantly, his death came a day after his benefit match had begun, the stoic participants opting to continue the contest wearing black armbands.

12  Twelfth Man

While most physical misfortunes befall cricketers in the midst of competition, some don't even get onto the field before disaster seeks them out. In 1921 A Dolphin fell off a chair in the Lord's dressing-room and broke a wrist. Should that appear to you to be a somewhat surreal occurrence, it should be pointed out that this was Arthur Dolphin, the Yorkshire wicketkeeper with eight championship victories to his rather unusual name and he had been reaching for his clothes at the time. Worse, though, is the growing volume of evidence to suggest that some cricketers are so inept that they can't even get as far as the ground before succumbing to injury. Trevor Franklin, the New Zealand batsman, is one, managing to get no further than the terminal building at Gatwick airport when he was run down by a motorised luggage trolley. But pride of place must go to Dereck Pringle and Don Topley, who proved that Essex Man, as most of us could have guessed, is not a man of letters. Pringle, despite going on to be cricket correspondent of two national newspapers, strained his back while penning a tome to a friend, while Topley was forced out of action as he went to post a package through a spring-loaded letterbox.

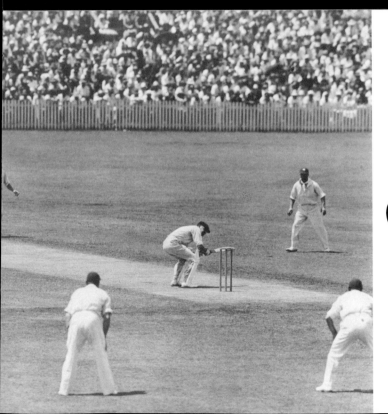

Chapter Eight

Worst

Gamesmanship

169

Worst Gamesmanship

I t has often been noted that cricket's ennobled view of itself is drawn from its reliance on Laws rather than simply rules. On the contrary, its dependence on such Laws merely confirms the suspicion that it is a game with little natural justice; from the toss, to the weather, to the pitch, to the side of the bed the umpire got out of in the morning, there is little respite from the cricketing fates. Indeed the scales, however often the cliché is used to try to ensure it, do not usually balance themselves out in the end. Add the human factor into the mix, and these Laws will often be stretched to their absolute limit, something that is occasionally referred to as gamesmanship (a more polite word than cheating). As a result of such behaviour, the Laws have become a work in progress, as the authorities seek to stay one step ahead of the miscreants. In truth, they are usually a couple of paces behind. For example, when batsmen caught on to the idea of using their legs as a second line of defence, the authorities hit back with the deterrent of the lbw Law. The game can absorb some of these activities, allowing them to exist in its fringes as long they don't try to force their way into the centre and spoil things for everybody. But sometimes they do, as the following examples, ranging from the spontaneous act of an individual to the considered tactics of a whole team, would suggest...

1

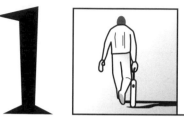

Trevor Chappell and Greg Chappell
Australia v New Zealand
Third One-Day International final. Melbourne. February 1981.

A BBC light entertainment programme once suggested that *Children Say the Funniest Things.* Maybe so, although the Ronnie Corbett-fronted show failed to provide definitive proof and was promptly dropped. But many a parent and bullied school pupil will tell you that they also manage to come up with the cruellest of comments, barbed jibes that hit you like a low blow in the abdominal protector and show all the sensitivity of a Steve Waugh sledge. It was one such comment that left Greg Chappell metaphorically writhing on the grass, grasping his nether regions. Chappell, who ordered his brother, Trevor, to bowl an under-

arm daisy cutter to prevent Brian McKechnie, New Zealand's chunky former All Black, from having any chance of hitting the six required to decide this game in his side's favour, was able to later shrug off taunts from the likes of Richie Benaud and Keith Miller that he was gutless and should be buried along with the corpse of one-day cricket; but the words of a nine-year-old girl, who ran on to the outfield shouting: "You cheated, you cheated," proved more difficult to dislodge. The New Zealand players were none too happy either, McKechnie hurling his bat down the pitch, Mark Burgess picking up the dressing room tea urn and smashing it against the wall; and captain Geoff Howarth racing out of the dressing-room to claim Chappell's action was against the rules (it was, but until then only in England), while the bemused non-striker Bruce Edgar proffered a two-fingered salute to nobody in particular.

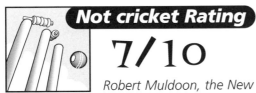

Not cricket Rating

7/10

Robert Muldoon, the New Zealand prime minister, was certain it was very much not cricket, climbing out of his bed in the middle of the night to lambast the incident as "the most disgusting in cricket history" before promising the Australians that if they "wanted it", they could have it "straight between the eyes". Late, in the only sound-bite he is ever remembered for, he opined that it was "appropriate the Australians had been wearing yellow". Chappell pleaded in mitigation that his judgement had been clouded after presiding over an exhausting schedule of five Tests and ten one-dayers before even getting to the best-of-five final. And he received unlikely support from a journalist from The Australian, who observed that Chappell hadn't ignored the traditions of the one-day game, because it was too young to have any.

2

Brian Rose
Worcestershire v Somerset
Benson and Hedges Cup. Worcester. May 1979.

It's the end of decidedly damp May, and your only sight of any people so much as resembling cricketers has been at the back of the pavilion as you've watched them splashing through the puddles on their way to their sponsored cars after another downpour has put an end to your latest futile wait for some play. But finally, as the month ends, you are woken by an unfamiliar shaft of light thrusting its way through the gap in your curtains. Hardly able to believe your good luck, not to mention your foresight in having booked the day off, you rise, rush off a few sandwiches, put the umbrella, with some emphasis, back in its stand by the front door, and with no little anticipation, hop on the bus down to the ground for a decisive limited-overs cup match. Newspaper in one hand, ale in the other, you excitedly take your seat. You have barely lifted your glass to your lips when the cry of no-ball from one of the umpires is followed by the bizarre sight of the opening batsmen trooping from the middle, an equally baffled bunch of fielders falling in behind them. After some moments of confusion, it is announced that the batting team have declared with their score on one for none. The other team knock off the two required to win, not surprisingly with little trouble. The spectacle has lasted little more than 20 minutes. As you ask around your fellow mystified

174

supporters, you learn that the captain of the team batting first has taken advantage of a competition rule that ensures his side's progression to the quarter-finals by denying his opponents the chance to increase their rate of taking wickets. The captain in this case was Brian Rose, of Somerset, and the unlucky 'winners' the home side, Worcestershire.

Not cricket Rating
9/10

Rose, a keen amateur gardener, found, somewhat fittingly, that he had dug himself into a hole so deep

even Charlie Dimmock would have given it up. But the captain was unrepentant. "We were almost certain to qualify, but we could have been overtaken by Worcestershire or Glamorgan. I had no alternative," he said. "My first duty is to Somerset and the rules were in black and white." He was about to discover they were a more curious shade of grey, as the TCCB machine sprang into action, voting Somerset out of the competition by 17-1. The MCC showed its own outrage by backing the expulsion, and only Derbyshire, strangely, played it by the book and supported Rose's case.

3

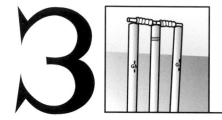

Javed Miandad
Australia v Pakistan
1st Test. Melbourne. March 1979.

Gardening, of course, is not just a hobby of some players – it has its own life as a cricketing term; to those unfamiliar with its meaning, it is that peculiar action you most often see a batsman taking between balls, especially if he has just played and missed, or the intended drive through mid-on has gone sailing over fourth slip. Not only does this strange patting – or, for the particularly stubborn divots, flat-batting – of the pitch suggest that the mistimed stroke is down to the vagaries of the playing surface rather than his own lack of skill, or the

bowler's abundance of it, it also helps to calm the nerves when the fearsome quickie has been muttering some choice phrases in his direction after he's sent his finest leg-cutter inadvertently to the third-man boundary. Even tail-enders like to imitate such customs, although they haven't really got a clue what they're doing. Rodney Hogg, for example, the Australian No 10 in this match against Pakistan, who played a rising ball into the off side before suddenly noticing a spot on the pitch that needed his immediate attention and setting off to deal with it. Hogg was never the most genial of characters on a cricket pitch, but then neither was the man standing at short leg: Javed Miandad. Miandad seized on the opportunity, skipped across the pitch behind Hogg's back to field the ball and threw down his wicket.

Not cricket Rating

4/10

The stranded batsman was not the only one to be amazed by

Miandad's action, and several of the Pakistan team sportingly called the befuddled Hogg back to the middle as he trooped off. But Hogg was to go from perplexed to vexed in a very short space of time when, as he prepared to resume his innings, umpire Clarence Harvey informed him that the decision had to stand. Hogg turned round and swatted two of his stumps out of the ground. Graeme Yallop, his captain, of the same mind that the ball should have been considered dead, observed: "I'm surprised he left one standing".

Allan Border
West Indies v Australia
One-Day International. Guyana March 1991.

Ian Chappell has become regarded as the Godfather of sledging, and while an opponent was not exactly likely to wake up face to face with a horse's head – barring a particularly lively night – they were liable to be exposed to some long, hard stares from the close field. And if the looks didn't kill, the language always might. Chappell's approach earnt his team the nickname The Ugly Australians, and, certainly, they have always seemed to prosper more under a leader with the gnarled quality of a man whose face has been carved from out the back of a

Gray Nicholls scoop than someone like Dave Gregory, the captain in their first Test match. Gregory, whose 6ft 2in frame and luxuriant black growth of beard meant he was often referred to as "Handsome Dave", was the prime example of the fact that Test matches are won by high pressure, not high cheekbones, and was discarded after three internationals. Steve Waugh is another who has subscribed to the Chappell diktat, happily watching opponents mentally disintegrate in front of his eyes, but what has made the Aussies champions in this dark art that lives and breathes at the very edge of acceptable cricket conduct is that attempts to outsledge them are doomed to failure. So it was, then, when Viv Richards took umbrage at Allan Border's decision to smash for six a delivery from Phil Simmons that slipped from his hands and bobbled slowly wide of the return crease. The Antiguan berated what he felt was his unsporting behaviour on three occasions afterwards, hoping that the guilt trip would upset Border's concentration. Unhappily for him though, Border used Richards's words to his own advantage, stating afterwards that he viewed the verbal barrage simply as a sign that cracks were appearing in the West Indies' proud exterior.

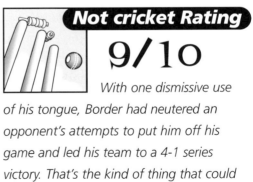

Not cricket Rating

9/10

With one dismissive use of his tongue, Border had neutered an opponent's attempts to put him off his game and led his team to a 4-1 series victory. That's the kind of thing that could get sledging a good name. Now that can't be allowed, surely?

5

Desmond Haynes
West Indies v England
3rd Test. Trinidad. March 1990.

Some people would say that international cricket, spread as it is over five days, is by definition a waste of time. What they would have made of the so-called timeless Tests, those in the early years of the game that were played to a definitive conclusion, is anybody's guess. Nevertheless, the speed of play is supposedly regulated under the formal Laws, and attempts by either the batting or fielding side to slow it down to gain an advantage are meant to be dealt with by the umpires under the heading of "unfair play". Desmond Haynes, however, proved superbly proficient in the technique when, with Viv Richards absent ill, he took charge of the West Indies for the first time, orchestrating a symphony of cynicism to prevent England taking a 2-0 lead in the series which, had anyone suggested the possibility before they left Heathrow, would have had him dragged off the plane as a danger to the flight. Devon Malcolm had set up the opening, his first ten-wicket haul in Test cricket leaving England to score 153 on the final day. But after Graham Gooch was forced to retire hurt and unseasonal rain washed out the middle session with the tourists on 73-1, Haynes and his merry band started to play. First was a Courtney Walsh solo, a single over that lasted nine minutes; it was followed by a staccato

180

interlude from Ian Bishop, who aborted two run-ups before complaining that it was too slippery for him to bowl; that led to an extended adagio section as Ezra Moseley ambled up to replace him, and a final improvised movement as Haynes waved substitutes on and off the field with helmets and spurious messages, and Jeff Dujon continually ran from his wicketkeeping position to offer advice to his captain. By the time they had concluded the piece, Bishop's final violent spell accounting for Allan Lamb, David Capel had to accept the second offer of bad light in the interests of safety with the score on 120 for five.

Not cricket Rating

8/10

Well, taking two hours over 17.5 overs requires some imagination and, let's face it, England would have tried to do the same in a similar situation. But the damage to the tourists' morale was done, and with Gooch out injured for the remaining two Tests, Curtly Ambrose and Bishop blew England away to claim a 2-1 series victory.

6

Tony Greig
West Indies v England
1st Test. Trinidad. February 1974.

There's nothing like an upbeat message from your leader to get you heading into a new year with optimism. And the Trinidadian Prime Minister's communication reported in the daily paper, the Trinidad Guardian, on New Year's Day 1974 was, indeed, nothing like an upbeat message. Dr Eric Williams took it upon himself to warn his people that there would be "little prosperity and much unhappiness" in the coming year, the worldwide energy crisis hitting the island's industry from garment manufacturers to road workers. While Dr Williams deserves credit for not delivering a googly to cover up the bad news, it was an outlook which had the local population desperately looking

for some light relief. And in Port-of-Spain, a couple of days into the first Test of England's tour to the Caribbean, it seemed as if they'd found some. The tourists had been summarily dismissed for a pitiful 131, and Alvin Kallicharran, the diminutive left-hander, had then struck a wondrous 142 not out, which was his score as he backed up at the non-striker's end with Derek Underwood bowling the final ball of the day to his Kent county colleague Bernard Julien. Julien competently pushed the delivery to short leg, turned to head for the pavilion, and was immediately followed by a number of fielders and Kallicharran. Enter Tony Greig, of whom one biography says "he was disposed to make wildly inappropriate moves on a spontaneous whim". This was one of those occasions, as he spotted that Kalli had not grounded his bat in his crease before departing. The future England captain hurled the ball at the middle stump and appealed for a run out. A slightly disorientated Douglas Sang Hue, the umpire, had no option but to rule in Greig's favour.

Not cricket Rating

5/10

It was within the rules, simply because there was no rule against it.

However, confusion reigned in the immediate aftermath, angry fans gathering outside the pavilion and demanding Kalli's reinstatement. After a meeting between the two captains and the respective managers, that is what they got. In a statement, the quartet said the appeal was being withdrawn "in the interests of cricket as a whole and this tour in particular". Kallicharran went on to make 158, and the hosts went on to complete a seven-wicket victory. Yet the pessimistic Dr Williams was to have the last word, as the teams returned to Trinidad for the fifth Test with England still 1-0 down in the series. The West Indies lost a close match and had to settle for that worst of all possible worlds, a shared rubber.

7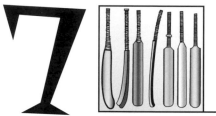

Two days before the start of this match, Greg Matthews, the Australia off-spinner, was wandering along a street in Georgetown with team-mate Mike Whitney and journalist Roland Fishman when he was set upon by a mugger, who ripped off a gold chain he was wearing. At least Matthews knew he had been the victim of daylight robbery, unlike Dean Jones whose wicket was snatched just as effectively. With the Aussies trailing by 221 on first innings, he'd made three from nine balls when Courtney Walsh produced an unplayable delivery which took out his middle stump. The death rattle from behind him had the effect of eclipsing the shout of no-ball from the mouth of C. Duncan, the umpire at the non-striker's end, and the Victorian started off up the pitch towards the pavilion believing his innings to be over. While Allan Border, his batting partner, tried frantically and in vain to alert Jones to what was unfurling, Carl Hooper moved in from the off side, gathered the ball, and with it in hand, uprooted another stump to claim the run out which the square leg umpire, Clyde Cumberbatch, believed he had no option but to confirm. It was only when a reporter from a press agency banged at their dressing-room door with a copy of the rules that the Australians began to realise that they'd been had. The Law governing appeals indicates that "the umpires shall intervene if satisfied that a batsman, not having been given out, has left his wicket under misapprehension that he has been dismissed". Too late. Australia were all out for 248, leaving the West Indies needing just a handful to win by ten wickets and take a 1-0 lead in the series.

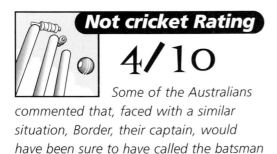

Not cricket Rating

4/10

Some of the Australians commented that, faced with a similar situation, Border, their captain, would have been sure to have called the batsman back. Border himself was not so sure, admitting that while it had been a "stupid dismissal", the notion of "unfair play" had never entered his mind. In the same circumstances, he said, "we'd have probably done the same thing". Viv Richards, the West Indies captain, suggested he had been ignorant of the law too, and only found out about it at tea on the fourth day, by which time "it was too late to do anything". The mood in the Australian camp, however, changed somewhat when word filtered through that most of the West Indians had not been as unfamiliar with the law as they had made out. Oh, and contacts with the local underworld enabled Matthews to get his chain back.

8

Dean Jones decided he wouldn't get mad, he'd get even: the Australians left the South American continent, heading first for St Vincent, for a tour match, and then for Trinidad, for the third Test. The flying between islands and the loss of two days' playing time to rain in Trinidad gave Jones plenty of time to catch up on some reading. Team-mates would find him holed up in the tail of a turbo-prop, or secreted in a quiet corner of the dressing-room, his head deep in some seemingly unfath-omable tome. In many ways it was unfathomable: it was the Laws of Cricket. Jones had become strangely fascinated by its contents, and his detailed study of Law 6 in particular was about to come in very handy in this warm-up match for the fourth Test in Bridgetown. In truth, Law 6, of all the Laws of the game, does not need too much study; it's quite simple really. The bat, it says, shall be no more than 38 inches in length, the blade shall be made of wood and shall not exceed 4.25 inches at its widest part. End of story. Well, it would have been, had not the eye that gave Jones such exceptional ability when the willow was in his hand registered something not quite right when Keith Arthurton arrived at the wicket. After the left-hander had played a few deliveries, Jones decided to share his misgivings with the umpires, who called immediately for the tape measure. This proved that the Windward Islander was using a bat 0.25 inches wider than was legal. Nevertheless, after some discussion, Geoff Marsh, the Australia captain, allowed Arthurton to continue using the implement.

Not cricket Rating

Mmmm. Motives may be everything in this situation. Arthurton later rejected claims of cheating, saying that tape he had wrapped round the blade to lengthen its life accounted for its increased width, but the addendum to Law 6 allows for only a sixteenth of an inch extra for such situations. Jones may have been upholding an important point, but only he will know if he really was concerned about applying the letter of the Law, or whether it was just tit-for-tat.

9  Douglas Jardine
Australia v England
1st to 5th Tests Sydney, Melbourne, Adelaide, Brisbane and Sydney again, November 1932 to February 1933.

Not so much leg theory as head and chest theory, Jardine's tactic, which spawned its own publishing industry, which still thrives 70 years after the event, not to mention a fiftieth anniversary BBC drama which highlighted the acting profession's ability to get to grip with the madness, if not the method, of the game, has become a byword for unsporting behaviour. Mention the term "bodyline" to an Australian male and you will see a man transformed in your presence more rapidly than the Incredible Hulk. If he doesn't actually turn green and burst out of his shirt, it is probably because his consumption of beer has done both of those things for him already. It will, at least, force him to go a particularly furious crimson and swell up with patriotic indignity. And all because of Jardine's determination to play the public school bully to Don Bradman's working-class hero and reclaim the Ashes snatched at the Oval in 1930. He persuaded Harold Larwood, in particular, to aim ferocious lifting deliveries at or just outside leg stump, and positioned a close leg-side field to snap up the chances as the batsmen tried to hook, pull or merely fend off balls which threatened life and limb. It worked a treat, and the Australians, with a couple of courageous exceptions, dropped like flies, and to a 4-1 series defeat. Even the dangerous Bradman had to be content with an average of 56, more than 40 runs below his career mark.

Not cricket Rating

Very much not cricket. Or, at least, that is the fiction. Jardine became a convenient focal point for Australian hatred, but in truth, relations between the two countries were strained in any case, partly because of trade hardships caused by the economic hangover of the Depression, partly because the Australian Board had refused to change the tour itinerary to allow England to fit in a couple of Tests in New Zealand ahead of seasonal rains. There is also a suggestion that Jardine didn't come up with the idea of bodyline on his own, but the files relating to the planning and execution of the tour mysteriously disappeared during the time Pelham Warner, joint manager of England in the 1932-33 series, took up residence as deputy secretary of the MCC.

189

10

Viv Richards
West Indies v England
4th Test. Barbados. March 1990.

Off-side, leg-side, Rob Bailey will probably go down as one of the few Test batsmen to have been caught off his backside. When a relatively harmless delivery from Curtly Ambrose flicked the Northamptonshire captain's buttocks on its way through to Jeff Dujon, the portly umpire Lloyd Barker seemed indifferent to the wicketkeeper's appeal. But Viv Richards's charge up the wicket, his voice raised and his fingers clicking, appeared to change Barker's demeanour and Bailey was sent on his way. Simply an umpire's error, then? Possibly, but a number of observers felt that something more sinister was at work, and suspicion was roundly focused on Richards and whether his over-zealous appealing had intimidated Barker into giving his decision. Christopher Martin-Jenkins was not the only one to intimate foul play – a number of Caribbean journalists were of the same opinion – but his response in his commentary that "if that's gamesmanship or professionalism, I'm not sure what cheating is" helped bring the pot of controversy nicely to the boil. Barker later claimed he had delayed his decision because he thought the batsman would 'walk', while Richards maintained that what others read as intimidation was just his performance of a "celebratory jig".

Not cricket Rating

The reaction provoked more controversy than the original action. Vic Fernandes, of Voice of Barbados Radio, mortified at what he considered Martin Jenkins' slur on Barbadians' "strong sense of fair play", banned the broadcaster from his station, while Barker initially issued a writ for defamation, sparking one other journalist to comment: "I hope Barker's lawyers don't read what I wrote."

11

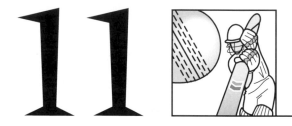

Dermot Reeve
Warwickshire v Hampshire
County Championship. Edgbaston. May 1996.

Throwing the bat is something usually associated with positive, even rashly adventurous, cricket. It is the action of a team trying to add late runs to boost their total, or the reaction of late-order players to imminent, and inevitable, defeat. Not, however, when that bat is in the hands of Dermot Reeve. Or, er, not in his hands, as in this instance. Rajesh Maru, Hampshire's left-arm spinner, was bowling into the rough outside Reeve's leg stump, and with plentiful turn and bounce from the footmarks was hoping to get the Warwickshire captain to glove a ball to one of the close fielders surrounding him. But the canny Reeve, noted for his ability to get up opponents' noses, and fighting to ensure a draw, remembered that a batsman could only be caught off his glove if the appropriate hand was still in contact with the bat at the time (Law 32 (i)) if you've got an hour or two). Now it gets really technical. With his chances of being out lbw nullified by Maru's trajectory outside leg stump, and his resultant use of the pad to prevent being bowled, he began to put the third part of a tactical master-plan – which he claimed he had once seen John Emburey use – into practice again, 15 times hurling his bat in the direction of silly point before Maru was forced to change his line of attack.

Not cricket Rating

2/10

Reeve's approach might have upset the purists, not to mention confused spectators and players without such adherence to the letter of the Laws. But it was a timely reminder of the benefits of studying the small print, although a number of newspapers got in a fervour and the MCC suggested the umpires could have given him out for obstructing the field (Law 37 (i)) or even handled ball (Law 33 (i)).

12

Twelfth Man

Some do it by nature, some view it as a duty to the game; some admit they do it only in certain circumstances, some that they do it only in certain forms of the game; others are reluctant to do it at all, perhaps because they are trying to balance a prior misfortune. Yes, we are, of course, talking about the contentious issue that historically has split the cricketing fraternity across the top, bottom and down the middle: the question of whether a batsman should "walk" when he knows he's out. Strangely, although it has become an accepted part of cricket mythology, the practice has never been as widespread as we have been led to believe, and while some observers reckon it harks back to the golden era of the amateur, plenty of evidence to the contrary has been provided to question that theory. Others have propounded that the act had a regional bias, the soft southern jessie being more liable to accept his fate than the grizzled northerner. Whatever, it is clear from the literature that it is a moral minefield, justifiable at one moment, indefensible the next. Yet, since any team or individual will buff themselves up into a lather of self-righteousness when a rival transgresses, it makes Ken Barrington's experience in South Africa in 1963-64 all the more outrageous. Having been ruled not out to a catch behind in the third Test, Barrington's conscience got the better of him and he walked off, only to be met the next day with headlines not hailing his sporting gesture, but condemning him for an ostentatious act of gamesmanship which held umpire Jack Warner up to ridicule.

Chapter Nine

The Worst

Dismissals

197

The Worst Dismissals

Many psychiatrists maintain that depression is the worst pain a human being can suffer, far worse than any of a physical nature such as that caused by being struck on the bridge of the nose by a speeding leather sphere propelled at upwards of 90mph. They are wrong. It is being run out. For 99. And that is why run-outs feature so prominently in the category that follows. However, it is far from being the only form of dismissal that can crack you square in the gut. There may only be ten official ways of getting out, but throughout the years players, from the finest opening batsman to the worst tailender, have created plenty of variations on the theme, and here are the most imaginative.

1

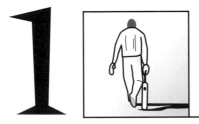

Harry Wilson
Northants v New Zealand
Tour match. Peterborough. June 1931.

While being run out for a duck may allow you to point to the absence of Lady Luck on a more important project, being run out for a duck twice hints at a complete deficit of either good fortune or judgment, two qualities just as significant as raw talent if you harbour serious ambitions of making it on the first-class stage. Doing it in the same match, however, against a touring Test team on your debut, suggests you would be better off seriously investigating other career avenues. Which, in fact, Harry Wilson was persuaded to do after his appearance at Peterborough was marked by such

disasters. The Northamptonshire committee did not feel that they needed a second opinion, casting the unfortunate Wilson into the cricketing wilderness following his quite appalling audition.

Outrageous misfortune or crass stupidity?

His bowling figures were none too impressive, either, and had he not captured the penultimate victim of the match, Milford Page donating his wicket as the New Zealanders romped home by six wickets, Wilson would have had a big fat round zero against his name there as well.

2

Mike Atherton
England v Australia
2nd Test. Lord's. June 1993.

All of us have experienced dreams in which our efforts to move or complete a task seem to be getting us nowhere, and there is no reason to expect that cricketers are any different in that respect. Fortunately, few of us have faced such a situation in waking life, especially not at Lord's and when our vision of a first Test century at the home of cricket is disappearing before our very eyes. Mike Atherton, however, did succumb to such a fate. He had reached 97 as, in partnership with Mike Gatting, he took England to 175 for two in the follow-on, still 252 adrift of making Australia bat again. With the whole crowd willing him to stroke the boundary that would relieve the tension and bring him that well-deserved hundred, Tim May turned at the Nursery End and ran in. Atherton clipped the ball off his hips and up the slope towards the deep mid-wicket area in front of the old Grandstand. It was a definite two, and yes, no, maybe – at a push – a three, and the promised land of three figures. But as Merv Hughes reached the ball and gathered it under the watchful eyes of Father Time – who, had you looked closely enough, might have been seen to crack a twisted smile as he got ready to witness the unfolding of yet another in a long line of English disasters – comfort gave way to indecision, the ground gave way beneath Atherton's feet as he terminated the attempt for a third and, after desperate efforts to get back up, he slipped again and was left floundering, like a man encased in quicksand, two yards out of his crease, making agonising, and vain, attempts to crawl back to safety before Ian Healy broke the stumps.

Outrageous misfortune or crass stupidity?

Comi-tragedy of which any playwright would be proud. Despite some resistance from Graeme Hick and Alec Stewart, England must have realised at this moment the game was up and Tim May, Shane Warne, and even Allan Border spun out the last four wickets for four runs.

3

Mark and Steve Waugh
Australia v England
5th Test. Perth. January 1995.

Twins are supposed to have an innate understanding, a quality that at its extreme can develop into what scientists identify as cry tophasia, a special language that only the pair of them understand. If the Waugh brothers, born within ten minutes of each other on June 2, 1965, had indeed invented their own form of communication as they grew up and followed each other into the New South Wales and Australia teams, the English fielders would have been treated to some interesting, if incomprehensible, vocabulary as the two walked off at the end of the Australia first innings. For Mark, acting as the injured Craig McDermott's runner, had left his (slightly) older sibling stranded on 99, by being run out.

Waugh (slightly) junior, presumably eager to see his elder brother reach the landmark (although sibling rivalry being what it is, it is hard to be completely sure), believed there was a single to be snatched as Steve dropped a delivery from Chris Lewis close to his own feet and looked imploringly towards the non-striker's end. However, something got lost in translation and while Steve was retracing his initial steps, Mark had put his head down and was motoring full pelt to the opposite end. When he noticed that his brother was no longer coming, he screeched to a halt, wheeled round and made a desperate attempt to scamper back, but was beaten by Graham Gooch's throw.

Outrageous misfortune or crass stupidity?

Mark's dismissal meant that Steve became only the second player to be left high, dry and 99 not out in a Test match, a fate first suffered by Geoff Boycott 15 years earlier.

4

Thomas Sidwell

Surrey v Leicestershire

County Championship. The Oval. August 1921.

Commuting on the capital's Underground system is a bit like a rite of passage; the Aborigines go Walkabout, Londoners try to get to High Barnet via Charing Cross without taking an unscheduled detour up the Bank branch-line. It's confusing enough for the locals, so imagine how disorientating it must feel when you don't originate from the Big Smoke – and the grid-like map we know today had yet to be invented. Thomas Sidwell, a native of Leicestershire, had been sent in as nightwatchman as his county

battled to stave off defeat at the Oval, but, after the close, he neglected to take adequate notice of his route to his overnight accommodation in Clapham. The following morning, the wicket-keeper, who had posted an undefeated single the night before, found the Tube network harder to negotiate than the Surrey bowling, and, when he passed Kennington for the third time, realised that he must be playing down the wrong line. When Sidwell hadn't arrived for the start, Leicestershire were forced to send in John King in his place.

Sidwell did finally find his way to the ground, but his troubles weren't over, for when he tried to resume his innings, Percy Fender, the Surrey captain, conferred with the umpires, who ruled that he should be considered out already. To be on the safe side, Surrey hurriedly consulted Lord's, who upheld the umpires' decision on the basis that Sidwell had not been kept away by illness or an accident. Surrey quickly wrapped up the match, the points keeping them in with a chance of denying Middlesex the title.

Outrageous misfortune or crass stupidity?

Misfortune; while the average Tube passenger may resent being squashed up against a neighbour's malodorous armpit while his train sits for 30 unexplained minutes deep in the bowels of the city, seething because he's already a quarter of an hour late for an important meeting, he can, unlike Sidwell, at least take comfort in the knowledge that his appearance at his workplace is unlikely to have a significant impact on the outcome of that year's county championship.

5

Sometimes, the crowd's reaction tells you all you need to know about a batsman's downfall, and the hush that descended over Trent Bridge when Geoff Boycott ran out Derek Randall on the second morning of this match could be heard the length and breadth of Nottingham. Randall was the local favourite, the clown, the trapeze artist, the eternal fidget; Boycott was the Yorkshire outsider, the strict ringmaster, the interminable bore, returning to the international cricket circus after three years of self-imposed exile. England had resumed at nine for no wicket in reply to Australia's first day

243, and there was no doubt whom the sellout crowd (with 5,000 locked outside) had really come to see. When Bob Woolmer quickly followed Mike Brearley back into the pavilion, Randall took to the stage to rapturous applause and seamlessly advanced to 13, a fine hooked four off Jeff Thomson offering promise of great things to come. However, as Boycott pushed a Thomson delivery just off to the leg-side of the mown part of the wicket, he had one of those rushes of blood so out of keeping with his character, and decided to try to pinch a single. Unfortunately, all Thomson had to do was abbreviate his follow through to pick the ball up, effectively blocking Randall in the process. By the time Randall had negotiated his way round the Australian bowler, the ball was in Rod Marsh's gloves, Boycott was safely at the non-striker's end and the hapless Randall was contemplating a return to the pavilion, the ever-present skip removed for once from his step.

Outrageous misfortune or crass stupidity?

Crass selfishness more like. Boycs, as ever, was looking after No 1, and, unfortunately for Randall,

No 4 came way down his list of priorities, although the Yorkshireman did have the decency to drop his bat by his side and hide his face behind his hands in shame. But the suspicion that these actions were merely crocodile tears survived, one journalist noting that "if the thought passed through Boycott's mind to turn back, it was soon gone". Not content with upsetting the locals, he went on to monopolise proceedings, making up for his long absence from Test cricket by batting on all five days of the match, while the century he recorded in a lengthy first innings marked the third time that he had run out an England team-mate and gone on to make a hundred.

6

Players in team sports have a saying to which they often make recourse when things are going badly for them in the Lady Luck department. "Who shagged the witch?" they say, as if to suggest that such an unwise union has brought a dreadful curse upon their dressing-room. If there's any truth in the adage, Michael Vaughan must have spent the early part of 2001 in an orgy at a Headingley coven. He missed a home Ashes series, and the first two Tests of the India tour, with maladies ranging from injuries to finger, wrist, calf and knee to a black eye and a dose of Delhi belly. When he did finally regain his place, in Bangalore on Graham Thorpe's return to England to sort out his own marital disharmony, he contrived to become the victim of a type of dismissal so rare it had happened only six times previously in 125 years of Test cricket. Vaughan had been batting beautifully in partnership with Mark Ramprakash, and had advanced to 64 when the left-arm spinner Sarandeep Singh bowled him one into his favoured sweeping zone. Shaping to play the stroke, he surprisingly failed to connect and as the ball looped up off his pad, getting tangled in a whirl of body, bat and gloves, and then down again,

Vaughan, still on one knee, inexplicably reached down and nudged it with his hand to the nearby short-leg fielder. The ball was not going to hit the wicket and it was unlikely to be caught, so there was a brief moment of indecision while all involved absorbed the implications of Vaughan's act. Eventually, Singh issued a belated, and slightly apologetic, appeal, and the umpire had no alternative but to give him out handled ball.

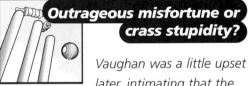

Outrageous misfortune or crass stupidity?

Vaughan was a little upset later, intimating that the Indians' appeal had been somewhat unsporting when he had only been trying to avoid inconveniencing the fielder by knocking the ball to him. But he got some revenge later, running out Sarandeep when India batted.

7

Len Hutton
England v South Africa
5th Test. The Oval. August 1951.

Batting was no easy task in this Test match, a surface particularly conducive to spin playing a major role in ensuring that 36 wickets fell in the three days it took to complete it. It was hardly the time, then, for one of England's greatest batsmen to compound problems by getting himself dismissed in a fashion never before seen in international cricket. The game had swung one way, then the other, until England had forged a position from which they needed only 163 to win in their second innings. Hutton and his partner, Frank Lowson, suggested there would be no cause for concern as they romped their way to 53 within 40 minutes. But the game changed again, for the penultimate time, as Hutton, on 27, opted to sweep against the off-breaks of Athol Rowan, who had a habit of snaring the best batsmen (perhaps as recompense for war wounds that left him bowling in leg irons); the Yorkshireman failed to make contact with the bat, but the ball ballooned upwards and behind him off his glove. Turning quickly, he swatted at it in an attempt to prevent it falling on the stumps, in the process hindering wicketkeeper Russell Endean's effort to catch it. A moment of silence and suspense was followed by an appeal and Hutton trooped off, a victim of obstructing the field.

Outrageous misfortune or crass stupidity?

An instinctive reaction rather than a wilful act, there is not enough evidence to convict of either. However, it could have had more serious repercussions. Hutton's dismissal saw England slump to 90 for four, and it was left to captain Freddie Brown, who had already been dropped three times, to throw caution to the wind and lead England to a four-wicket victory which ensured a 3-1 win rather than a shared series.

8

Charles McLeod
Australia v England
1st Test. Sydney. December 1897.

Cricket is a hard enough game when you are in possession of all your senses; when you are deprived of one of them, it becomes even more daunting. It was a wonder, then, that Charles McLeod, who was afflicted by partial deafness, was able to reach first-class level at all, let alone the Test stage, where he scored a century and four fifties in his 17 matches, and took 33 wickets. His returns from his batting might have been even more impressive had his condition not made him a nightmare to run with between the wickets. Yet if any of his resulting run-outs were to leave a particularly sour taste, it was this one, as England took unforgivable advantage of McLeod's impairment. Batting at No 3 as Australia followed on, he had helped his side to 135 for one when Tom Richardson, the England quickie, bowled him a high full toss. Mistaking the shout of no-ball from the umpire for the non-striker Joe Darling yelling "Look out", McLeod backed away and was bowled. Thinking he was out, he started to walk off, upon which Bill Storer, the wicketkeeper, pulled out the stump and claimed the run out instead.

Outrageous misfortune or crass stupidity?

A mixture of bad luck and malevolence, Storer claimed to Clem Hill, the batsman who replaced the unfortunate Victorian, that he "would not have had that happen for 20 dollars". During the lunch interval he sought out McLeod, explaining that he had been told to break the wicket and "it was only when the wicket was down that I realised the position". So sorry was the stumper that he took the Australian his favourite bat and said he could have it. His regret was so genuine that in the end even McLeod got fed up with it and told him to go away and forget about it.

9

Trescothick
Sri Lanka v England
3rd Test. Colombo. March 2001.

O ne day in the early 1990s, and obviously finding themselves with too much time on their hands, two professors from Oxford and Sussex universities decided to fill their schedule by trying to work out a mathematical formula for a fielder taking a catch on the run. After detailed study of several Test match videos, they pronounced it to be $d^2 (\tan a)/dt^2 = 0$. For the algorithmically disinclined, the most critical aspect of the theorem was the 'a' – the angle of elevation of gaze from catcher to ball. What practical application this may have had is unclear; it would certainly have been of little use to Russel Arnold, the Sri Lankan stationed at short leg as Marcus Trescothick waited to receive from left-arm spinner Dinuka Hettiarachchi. He would definitely have had little opportunity to calculate the elevation of his gaze as the beefy left-hander eyed up a slog sweep, except to note that it was fixed on a spot somewhere between his groin and his ankle as he thrust his arms over his head and tried to turn himself into a smaller target. When he did finally chance to lift his eyes upwards again he was no doubt surprised to find that the ball, far from taking his head off and propelling it towards the square leg boundary at the velocity of a rifle bullet, had actually come to rest in the copious folds of his loose-fitting shirt. He was also able to

make out Trescothick disappearing towards the pavilion desperately trying to fathom the sequence of events that had led to his downfall.

Outrageous misfortune or crass stupidity?

Looking back, Trescothick could count himself doubly unlucky: he was one of only two victims of Hettiarachchi, who was making his debut and has not added to his haul for the simple reason that he has never again been picked.

215

Bernard Hedges and Willie Jones

Glamorgan v Sussex

County Championship. Llanelli. July 1951.

Hedges and Jones are not names that roll off the tongue like Morecambe and Wise, but the comedy double act they contrived on the final afternoon of an inevitable draw certainly brought some sunshine into the lives of a meagre and soporific crowd. Maybe something was slipped into their salads, but within a minute of the luncheon interval, Glamorgan lost a wicket in what the South Wales Evening Post described as "a most peculiar fashion". Hedges pushed a ball towards mid-wicket and called for a quick single; with both pairs of eyes concentrating on the ball as they raced for their respective ends, the duo collided violently in mid-pitch, Jones

being knocked out cold, and a prone and somewhat dizzy Hedges watched in bewilderment as the Sussex fielders, showing professionalism and then humanity, ran him out before lifting his fallen comrade and carrying him back to the pavilion.

Outrageous misfortune or crass stupidity?

Has to be placed firmly in the stupidity section as Sussex, through no ability of their own, managed to kill two birds with one stone, although the record shows that Jones returned to complete an unforgettable innings of 31.

11

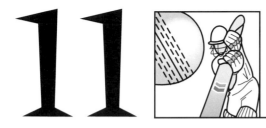

Alan Revill
Surrey v Derbyshire
County Championship. The Oval. June. 1953.

In the psychology of batsman/fast bowler relationships, the former are usually advised to hide their pain when the latter leaves them desperate to wring the soreness out of whatever part of their anatomy has been assaulted; this important mental aspect of the game had obviously not been sufficiently impressed on Derbyshire's Alan Revill. Struck on the hand by a lifting ball from Alec Bedser, Revill shook it extravagantly, and watched in dismay as his glove flew off and dislodged a bail. He was adjudged out hit wicket.

Outrageous misfortune or crass stupidity?

Little sympathy for the batsman, who paid a high price for his display of wimpishness.

Twelfth Man

Not quite a worst dismissal, but worthy of inclusion simply on the basis of intent, is an incident originating in the second Test between England and India at Old Trafford in 1936, courtesy of the visiting team's captain, Sir Gajapatiraj Vijaya Ananad, the Rajkumar of Vizianagaram. With a name like that, you might have guessed that he ingratiated himself with the British Raj, if not the master of ceremonies at their dinners at which he was a frequent guest, but Vizzy, as he became more familiarly known, did like to take things to extremes, even employing two servants to tie his bootlaces and help him put his pads on. His political skills, rather than any great cricketing ability, earned him the Indian captaincy in the first place, so it was really no surprise when Vijay Merchant, widely regarded as his nation's first outstanding Test batsman, asked Vizzy, on the eve of the previous Test, to stand down in the interests of his country. Needless to say, Vizzy declined the invitation, and India went on to lose by nine wickets, but he didn't forget about it. As Mushtaq Ali and Merchant compiled a large partnership in Manchester, Vizzy was in the dressing-room, plotting his revenge. Mushtaq duly completed his century and, on returning to the pavilion at lunch, Vizzy craftily put his plan into action, garlanding him with praise, presenting him with a gold wristwatch as a reward – then ordering him to run out Merchant before he could get his hundred. Fortunately, the story has a happy ending. Mushtaq proved he could not so easily be bought, refusing to carry out Vizzy's demand and informing Merchant about it as they resumed their partnership in the afternoon session: Merchant defiantly reached three figures, leaving Vizzy to take his temper out on his unfortunate valets.

Chapter Ten

Worst
Off-field
Crimes and
Misdemeanours

Worst off-field crimes and misdemeanours

While many players are happy for their demons to go on public display (see chapters two and three), others prefer to be more circumspect, carrying out their sometimes dubious, sometimes disgusting and occasionally disgraceful antics away from the intrusive glare of television, the newspapers, or their wives. However, the modern media frenzy is such that the slightest sniff of scandal can turn even the most slothful journalist into a ravenous beast. Even cricketing heroes of long ago are no longer safe, as studious and, yes, slightly sadistic biographers trawl the libraries for a trace of what they really got up to on those six-week-long sea crossings to and from the Antipodes. And, more dangerous still, since some of the subjects are long dead, the writers are not bound by libel laws...

1

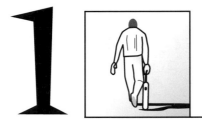

Ed Pooley
Surrey
May 1877.

In these days of saturation coverage, Nasser Hussain has to content himself with a three-fingered salute to the occupants of the Lord's media centre when responding to caustic discharges from their laptops. Pooley, a wicketkeeper of some repute, preferred a more direct approach. On this occasion, scathing Sporting Life scribe EH Pickering found himself backed up against the bar at the Oval, and offered a shilling for the honour of having his lights punched out for describing one of Pooley's innings as "devoid of elegance". Pooley, who fathered eight illegitimate children, was also unable to take his place in the first Test in history in Melbourne after being detained in a New Zealand cell following a brawl connected to a bizarre gambling debt. Having forecast the scores of four Canterbury batsmen, Pooley donned the umpire's coat because he was injured, and gave the hapless foursome out.

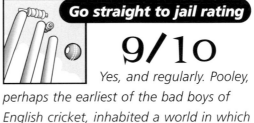

Go straight to jail rating

9/10

Yes, and regularly. Pooley, perhaps the earliest of the bad boys of English cricket, inhabited a world in which laws, whether of the land or of the game, were there to be broken.

2

Julius Caesar
Surrey and England
October 1865.

To the uninitiated, the town of Godalming, situated picturesquely on the River Wey, might seem like any other sleepy Surrey backwater, remarkable only for its ordinariness and its proximity to its bigger city brother of Guildford. But scratch the surface, and this small suburban setting reveals a somewhat more disconcerting underbelly. One such underbelly was that belonging to Mary Tofts, who, in 1726, legend has it, gave birth to 18 rabbits – only a few more than spawned by English cricket in an average Ashes series. But The Rabbit Woman of Godalming, as she unambiguously became known, is not the town's only claim to notoriety: a couple of centuries later, in 1912 to be exact, it was forced to wave a solemn goodbye to John 'Jack' Phillips, a favourite son who had made the poorest of career choices in becoming chief wireless operator on the Titanic. However, the most tragic figure to emerge from its womb must surely be the 19th century Surrey and England cricketer Julius Caesar. Like the Roman version in name alone, the extent of Caesar's ambition, despite his diminutive stature, was to dictate to opposition bowlers, although this early practitioner of the pull shot must have felt a burgeoning identity crisis deepen when his team-mates insisted on referring to him as 'Julie'. His nervous disposition would hardly have been helped, then, when, at the age of 35, he accepted an invitation to a shooting party that went spectacularly,

and fatally, awry. Stumbling on a muddy bank in the rain, he inadvertently set off the trigger on his rifle and bagged an accompanying gamekeeper instead of a pheasant.

Go straight to jail rating

3/10

The inquest accepted it was an accidental death, but additional traumas including the suicide under a passing train of his lovelorn son, Julius junior, left poor Caesar fit for little but withering away in isolation and relative poverty in a small room above a pub in his native town.

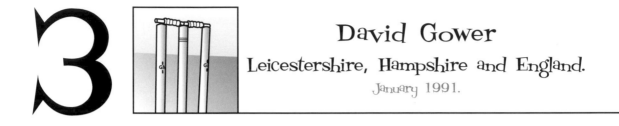

3

David Gower
Leicestershire, Hampshire and England.
January 1991.

For those raised on the question-able sporting amusement of the BBC panel show *They Think It's All Over* (and, thank God, for this former England captain it does now appear to be), where the rapid silvering of Gower's curly locks earned him the dubiously genial epithet of "The Old Lady", it may be hard to appreciate that the now Sky commentator was once a dashing golden boy in the England middle order, who would gracefully align a Gray Nicholls scoop of Potteresque properties with passing bullets from the likes of Marshall, Holding and Ambrose, while effusing the sang-froid of a British agent mixing a cocktail as he's dangled over a shark-infested swimming pool. It was an admirable coolness that was to get him into trouble – and not only outside the off stump. Tiring of the tyrannical practice sessions imposed by captain Graham Gooch during the England tour of Australia in 1990/91, he took advantage of an up-country game in Careera, Queensland, to give full rein to his imprisoned spirit. Recovering in the pavilion after a typically exacting 20 minutes in the middle, his gaze fell upon a small grassy airfield across the road from the ground, where a local Red Baron was preparing to give visitors to this Gold Coast playground a couple of circuits of the arena in an old Tiger Moth. Grabbing some goggles and a naive and impressionable team-mate in John Morris, he talked the pilot into taking them on a low-level water bombing raid, which dampened a prosperous England partnership between Allan Lamb and Robin Smith.

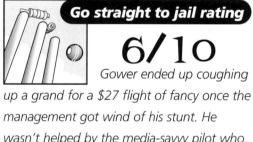

Go straight to jail rating

6/10

Gower ended up coughing up a grand for a $27 flight of fancy once the management got wind of his stunt. He wasn't helped by the media-savvy pilot who, spotting a good photo opportunity, had alerted a number of snappers, and they were waiting to turn their flashbulbs on the Leicestershire miscreant as he stepped, grinning and with barely a hair out of place, from the cockpit. Morris merely never played for England again.

4

Richard Wardhill
Victoria
August 1873.

Many of the convicts arriving in Australia with the First and Second Fleets were in such bad condition after the 12,000-mile journey that they were unable to walk. It's a characteristic that's been passed down from generation to generation of Aussie batsmen. Whether it's nicking the ball to the wicketkeeper or a sack of potatoes from an 18th century London market stall, they've decided dishonesty is the best policy. Or, as in the case of Dick Wardhill, the first centurion in Australian first-class cricket (110 for Victoria v New South Wales in 1867) embezzling $7,000 from his employers, the

Victoria Sugar Company, to cover mining investment and gambling losses. At least he had some shame: confronted with the extent of his fraud, he owned up and agreed to accompany the firm's directors to a Melbourne police station; on the way they acceded to his request to be allowed first to call at his home to explain all to his family. Once there, he slipped out the back door, made hurriedly for the River Yarra, and threw himself in. It was three days before his body was recovered.

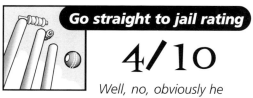

Go straight to jail rating

4/10

Well, no, obviously he didn't. Like Wardhill, some Australians have tried to play down their ancestors' criminal pasts. For others, though, it's been a source of considerable pride. In the early 1970s, a Sydney newspaper published the surnames of all the convicts on the First and Second Fleets, and offices in the city emptied as workers raced to the news-stands to see if theirs was on the list.

5

Mike Gatting
Middlesex and England
June 1988.

In the panoply of unlikely sporting conquests, Mike Gatting's ability to persuade a barmaid to return to his hotel quarters for a spot of room service on the eve of the first Test against the West Indies in Nottingham in 1988 probably yields only to David Mellor and his faculty for becoming a sexually-appetising prospect to a Spanish actress by dressing up in a Chelsea kit. Actually, considering the lardy former Middlesex and England captain's fondness for all things fry up and tuck, it would not be surprising if the latter-day Maid Marian had got the wrong end of the breadstick when he whispered in her ear that she might like to "go upstairs" for something sweet.

Whatever, Gatting's hospitality was not returned by his TCCB employers at breakfast the following Sunday morning, when the story got its sordid spin in the tabloids. They made it clear that, as far as leading his country was concerned, he was toast.

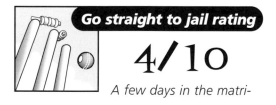

Go straight to jail rating

4/10

A few days in the matri- monial doghouse was probably as severe as it got for Gatting, for whom months of porridge would have been interminable agony. His removal as England captain, however, had been a formality waiting to happen since his contretemps with Shakoor Rana the previous winter. Ian Botham was not convinced by Gatting's supposed sexual shenanigans, though. "Anything that goes into his bedroom after 10pm, he usually eats," was his confirmation of the stereotype.

6

Across between a cricketer and a Chippendale, Chris Lewis, the England all-rounder once touted as a successor to Ian Botham, was one of that particularly curious brand of sportspeople who insist on talking about themselves in the third person. You know the type: asked a question about their future, for example, they will reply with something along the lines of: "Chris Lewis will do what's best for Chris Lewis," leaving the assembled journalists scratching their heads and wondering if they were talking about someone completely different. It is this strange narcissistic approach to his own identity that probably led him to suffer serious sunburn during practice in the Caribbean when he shaved his head, be rather too quick to do a full monty for the discerning readership of Playgirl, and feel he was an outcast at Nottinghamshire because he wore the wrong kind of underwear (Calvin Klein, if you're interested). The finest example of such self-inflicted misfortune, though, came when he failed to report for duty in time for the Sunday of the final Test against Pakistan at the Oval in 1996. The excuse that his Mercedes had sustained a puncture on Vauxhall Bridge, and that he couldn't let anyone know because the battery on his mobile had run out, cut little ice with the England management, who remained convinced he just hadn't got out of bed in time.

Go straight to jail rating

Despite pleading his case with a letter to The Times, Lewis was left out of the squad to tour in the winter.

7

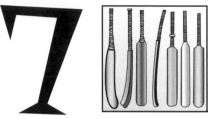

Shane Warne
Victoria, Hampshire and Australia
February 2003.

Controversy has followed Shane Warne like one of his top-spinners spearing in to trap an unsuspecting batsman plumb in front on the back foot: there have been the reports of sexy mobile phone calls to nurses and exotic dancers in various parts of the globe, the photographs of him furtively puffing on a cigarette while being sponsored to give up smoking, and the example of him providing, along with team-mate Mark Waugh, information on the pitch and the weather to an Indian bookmaker. All in all, you could say that, like a poorly-directed flipper, he has not always managed to stay on the straight and narrow. He would seem, in fact, just the kind of person who could benefit from a bit of parental guidance. Or perhaps not. A number of Australian cricketers, despite their macho reputations, have turned out to be unconscionably close to their mums: Ian and Greg Chappell's would play umpire to their boyhood backyard Tests, while the 13-year-old David Boon used to present his with his precocious architectural drawings for approval. But the low-fat version of the allegedly vain Warne, who had slimmed down from a 36in to 32in waist in 12 months, will have wished he had not taken his mum's advice to take one of her diet pills so he would look good for a press conference shortly before the 2003 World Cup in South Africa: the tablet was a diuretic prohibited because of its ability to mask other banned substances.

Go straight to jail rating

4/10

He might as well have. Withdrawing from the World Cup, he flew back to Australia, where an Australian Cricket Board hearing failed to be convinced by his arguments for taking the pill, and suspended him for one of a possible two years. Unable to take up a £250,000 contract to skipper Hampshire in the subsequent English summer, things got so bad that at one point, according to reports, he even considered trying to qualify to play for the Poms.

8

Phil Tufnell
Middlesex and England
January 1991.

Not so much *I'm a Celebrity... Get me Out of Here* as *I'm a Celebrity and This is More Fun Than Playing Cricket for a Living, Actually.* Which is strange, considering that it is an enduring belief that the former Middlesex and England spinner would have ended up serving some time at Her Majesty's Pleasure, if not confined behind the walls of a high-security hospital, but for the sanctuary that the game provided. Nevertheless, it was a security that he was regularly happy to put on the line, and now, with the extraordinary literary work *Phil Tufnell's A-Z of cricket*, (B is for Bird and not of

the Dickie variety; T is for Tits, not Turn, and so on) his sins – many of which, it has to be said, read like a revival of a Brian Rix farce sexed up for the *Big Brother* generation – are finally paying dividends. Certainly, sexed up is what Tuffers must have been feeling when he decided to indulge in a *menage a cinq* ahead of a one-day international in Adelaide. Lured back to the apartment of four boozy blondes, he was understandably disconcerted when a malfunctioning alarm clock caused him to miss the meeting time for the players' journey from the team hotel to the Adelaide Oval the next morning. When

Robin Smith offered a perturbed Mickey Stewart the unlikely but inspired excuse that Tufnell preferred to jog down to the ground in the morning, it appeared that his bases were covered. However, Smith had reckoned without Tufnell's unerring sense of slapstick and comic timing. Rushing into the hotel foyer, and reckoning he could still make the ground within half an hour, he grabbed the keys to his room, sped carelessly across the newly-polished floor, slipped and ended flat on his back in front of the lift just as the management team of Stewart, Peter Lush and Graham Gooch, delayed in leaving, emerged.

Go straight to jail rating

3/10

Charmed life or what? Tufnell would probably be best suited to a part in Survivor, the ITV reality show that bombed despite featuring the immaculately-coiffured Channel 4 cricket luvvie Mark Nicholas as its frontman. Fined just £500, he went on to star in some classic sequels in which he briefly ended up in a Perth psychiatric hospital (I'm an England Cricketer... Let Me Out of Here), got clobbered with a brick by his ex-girlfriend's father, and got set up by a New Zealand restaurant in a drug-inspired PR stunt.

9

Wally Hammond
Gloucestershire and England
April 1926.

O ne of the finest English cricketers of his – or any – generation, Hammond looked more like Phil Tufnell after a night out with the Barmy Army as he staggered from the ship returning the England team to these shores following the tour of the Caribbean in 1926. Early on in the trip, he had begun to suffer from a fever, weight loss, and myriad other symptoms which no one seemed able to put together into an acceptable diagnosis and he spent much of the time in bed, hallucinating and barely able to talk. For many years, his illness remained wrapped in mystery and understatement, as Jamaica's much-maligned mosquitoes took most of the blame for his condition. In print, Hammond identified it

238

as a form of blood poisoning; later biographers have sought a second opinion, though, modern medicine giving credence to the view that the venerable Wally had contracted something altogether more venereal. It is not too far-fetched a theory, for the truth was, Wally, a shy chap with his teammates, saved his charm for the ladies, and liked to put it about a bit. In an unusual variation on the village cricket tradition, which sends a collection hat around spectators to show their appreciation of a landmark such as a century, he was even offered the services of a large, dark woman of the night after an undefeated innings of 238.

Go straight to jail rating

2/10

It wasn't criminal, but it was risky. Hammond lost a whole English season as he was confined to a nursing home.

"**B**OTHAM BONKS MOTHER THERESA" is a headline that fortunately failed to make it as far as the deranged imagination of even a *Daily Sport* editor, let alone print, but it says something about the media treatment of the biggest flawed hero of the 20th century (Botham, that is, not Mother Theresa) that he should feel it necessary to suggest in his autobiography, oh-so-naughtily subtitled *Don't Tell Kath*, that it could have done. Sir Len Hutton once described the all-rounder as the first rock 'n' roll cricketer. Well, rock 'n' roll, in truth, may not have been top of the Beefy agenda – if you discount a friendship with the trout-lipped cricketing fanatic Mick Jagger and the extenuating circumstances that led him to trash a hotel room with a pizza – but sex and drugs, if you believe what you read, certainly were. But if the drugs didn't lack substance – he was forced to admit in a newspaper article that he had lied about trying cannabis – the sex (supposedly with Lindy Field, a former Miss Barbados during the West Indies tour in 1986) may have done, the purported breaking of his bed during their alleged nocturnal fusion being explained more prosaically by virus-ridden room-mate Les Taylor, the Leicestershire trundler, collapsing on it. Accusations of assault also failed to pass detailed scrutiny; he was supposed to have lamped a policeman three times on one of his charity walks (no charges were pressed); he was supposed to have thumped Steven Isbister in a Scunthorpe alleyway after the naval rating had got into a scrap with a mate (he was acquitted at Grimsby Crown Court); even a 67-year-old grandmother spoke up for him when a passenger intervened in a rowdy Queensland selection meeting between Botham, Allan Border and Greg Ritchie on an Ansett flight (he was found technically guilty, after implying that the aggrieved traveller should mind his own business and should rotate his head 180 degrees).

OK, so he did destroy a Tasmanian dressing-room in combination with Dennis Lillee, but every player has to let off a bit of steam now and then, surely.

Go straight to jail rating

6/10

An unhealthy amount of hit, no doubt, but also a liberal helping of myth. Botham may have been no angel, and he certainly overnighted in a variety of cells, but many of his off-field exploits have been as much the product of creative writing, in an ultimately destructive war of the tabloids, as his own boorish behaviour.

241

11

Terry Jenner
South Australia, Western Australia, Cambridgeshire and Australia September 1988

When Terry Jenner was led down an Adelaide prison corridor to start his stretch of six-and-a-half years for embezzlement, he noticed how the other inmates lining the way to witness his walk of shame all had beards and appeared rather angry and aggressive; at that moment he must have realised what it was like for an English batsman walking out to make his debut in an Ashes series. It is a tale related in the Australian's autobiography, which, by including a separate index devoted to his fellow lags (among them Frankie, Woody, Johnny and Ronnie), sets it apart from most of this genre. Jenner never quite fulfilled his promise as a leg-break bowler, playing only nine Tests, but the wrist-spinner's tendency to back himself was to prove his downfall, and, when the money to fund his gambling addiction dried up, he swiped A$10,000 from his employer and was sent down, condemned by the judge as "a parasite". An early meeting with a man who had cut off his wife's head encouraged him to keep his own down, but his attempts to maintain a low profile were scuppered when he was made captain of the 'Billabong Hilton's' cricket team, a role that put him in the unenviable position of explaining to a mass murderer why he had been left out of the first XI.

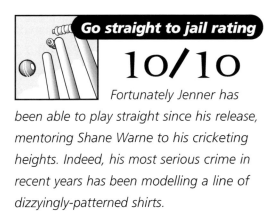

Go straight to jail rating

10/10

Fortunately Jenner has been able to play straight since his release, mentoring Shane Warne to his cricketing heights. Indeed, his most serious crime in recent years has been modelling a line of dizzyingly-patterned shirts.

12 Twelfth Man
Adam Parore

Martin Crowe was driving with his girlfriend to Newcastle Airport at the end of the tour to England in 1990 when he was stopped in his tracks by a horrifying sight along one of the winding country lanes on the route. There, in a ditch to the side of the road, lying on its side and slightly crumpled, was a red New Zealand sponsors' Ford Sierra, the bold white lettering across the doors displaying the legend Sir Richard Hadlee. Shocked as he was, he didn't immediately fear for the safety of his country's recently appointed cricketing knight, who had signed off his international career with eight wickets at Edgbaston a few days earlier. He was however, concerned for the wellbeing of Adam Parore, who had made his debut in that same match. Parore had borrowed Hadlee's car for the trip and when Crowe could find no evidence of the 19-year-old, who had just become his country's youngest-ever Test wicketkeeper, in the car or in the surrounding fields, he began to sweat. He needn't have worried; while he was busy shepherding away a party of Japanese tourists excitedly waving their cameras in the direction of the wreckage, Parore was already airborne. After scrambling clear, and taking his cricket equipment from the boot, Parore had flagged down a passing tractor and persuaded the farmer driving it to take him to the airport. Crowe would not even have seen the wreckage had the farmer not pocketed the hundred quid Parore had given him, and failed to keep his part of the deal of retrieving the vehicle and taking it to a nearby garage. But Parore, nicknamed Maverick in light of the incident and who was later to become a controversial figure in his country's cricket (run-ins with national and provincial coaches were followed by having the title of world's worst sledger bestowed on him by none other than Shane Warne), had learnt an important lesson, applicable as much to his cricket life as his time behind a wheel: a moment's inattention can be costly. The Aucklander admitted the crash had happened as he took his eye off the road to change the station on the car radio.

Chapter Eleven

The Best of
the Rest of
the Worsts

The Best of the Rest of the Worsts

And so we reach the post-tea session, when, by rights, we should be winding down, taking stock – and few chances. We should be seeing off the second new ball, playing for the morning when we will be fresher and can continue to build our innings. But, you know, you just can't do that these days, since Australia reinvented the approach to batting. You have to be positive at all times, and woe betide you if you're not averaging about 4.73 an over by the close of play. So with that in mind, here are the best of the rest of the worsts, a pot-pourri of early-evening shots, some, like a cultured drive, played with a fairly straight bat, others, like a reverse sweep that doesn't quite come off, of dubious merit...

1

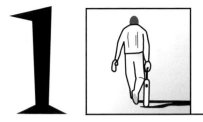

Worst Gambler
Hansie Cronje in India

Some people think that the exposure of the match-fixing activities of Hansie Cronje, Salim Malik and Mohammad Azharuddin (to name the three best known to have been tapped up by dodgy bookmakers) robbed cricket of its virginity, but the making of ill-gotten gains was a part of the game even before 1881 when three England cricketers were accused of being paid to under-perform against Victoria, and the 1920s, when England captain Lionel Tennyson won a Rolls Royce from a friend in a flutter over how long it would take a fly on his windscreen to defecate. Anyone who can afford to lose a prized motor on such a whim can probably absorb the forfeiture, but it is hard to believe that the leather jackets and financial incentives that were offered to Cronje, the born-again Christian, were suitable compensation for gambling with a career that had made him practically a deity in the post-apartheid South Africa that he captained. However, as he was to testify to the King Commission, his religious technique, adopted after he had mown down a six-year-old child in a road accident, had proved as fallible as a batsman probing into the corridor of uncertainty: by the end of it he had admitted he had taken his eye off Jesus and at least $100,000 in bribes from Indian bookmakers.

2

Worst Over (part one)
Robert Vance,
Canterbury v Wellington
Shell Trophy, Christchurch, February 1990.

A picture may paint a thousand words, but a series of numbers can create a pretty damning portrait, especially when the canvas is a cricket scorebook, and your only entry in it is one over for 77 runs. In fact, so impressively bad was Robert Vance's effort in this four-day match that it should have been framed and plastered on the Christchurch pavilion wall as an example of how not to make a game of it. Yes, almost inevitably, this over was an example of one of the leading forms of anti-cricket – the attempt to contrive a result from a match that looks set for a draw – Vance being urged by his skipper, Ervin McSweeney,

to bowl no-balls to encourage the Canterbury batsmen, who had pulled up the footbridge and taken refuge in defence after being reduced to 108 for eight, to continue to pursue an unlikely target of 291. Lee Germon was the chief beneficiary, wearing out three of the scorer's HB pencils as he pillaged eight sixes, five fours and a single in the 22-ball over, being caught twice off no-balls. (His partner Roger Ford's share was just six.) Bizarrely, having drawn level with Wellington's score, the Canterbury batsmen responded in a similar vein of insanity, refusing to take the single off the final ball that would have won them the match.

3 Worst Over (part two)
Surrey v Derbyshire
County Championship. The Oval. June. 1953.

David Hill, the Guyanese off-spinner, loved to bowl so much that he wasn't going to let the shocking inability of an unnamed umpire to count to put him off his stride. In the second of two consecutive five-day matches, played between the islands in Georgetown in the era of eight-ball overs, he managed to send down an over of 14 deliveries that included no wides or no-balls. Everton Weekes had failed to draw the umpire's attention to the error as he helped himself to a fifty, but he might have preferred it if he had, for when the 14th clipped him on the pads, the umpire was decisive enough to give him out. Obviously the appeal had brought him to his senses and as Weekes wandered off, he finally managed to compose the word "over" and strolled contentedly off towards square leg.

251

4

Worst Pitch
Sabina Park, Jamaica,
West Indies v England
1st Test, January 1998.

" It's Saturday, it's eight o'clock and it's the Lottery." It was an appropriate choice of words with which England opener Alec Stewart welcomed Nasser Hussain to the crease early on the first day of this series, even if it was a Wednesday and nearly 11 in the morning, for Michael Atherton and Mark Butcher were already back in the dressing-room – in all honesty, the safest place to be. What's more, when Hussain took guard and looked up, he would have seen, in the distance at the end of his run-up, a sight more terrifying than an angry Curtly Ambrose: a grinning one. The Antiguan had good reason for the unusual jocularity that had replaced his

more familiar murderous countenance: he had no idea whether the next ball he bowled would leap off a good length and brush past Hussain's left ear as he exercised his forward defensive, or scuttle through at metatarsal height, snapping at the Englishman's ankles en route to the middle stump; and if Ambrose had no idea, the batsman was in seriously big trouble. Three overs into the match, Srinivasaraghavan Venkataraghavan, one of the umpires, had already got on his walkie-talkie to match referee Barry Jarman, to express his reservations about a pitch whose undulations had been exposed before play by the England management stretching a piece of string between the two sets of stumps. By the time Stewart had taken several blows to his highly-protected person, and Wayne Morton, the England physio, had more or less taken up residence on the field, everyone had seen enough. Atherton was summoned onto the field to discuss the situation with Brian Lara, his opposite number, the umpires, and Jarman; before long, the decision to abandon a Test because of the state of the pitch was taken for the first time in 1,396 matches. There had been less than an hour's play. The fault was with the Jamaican Cricket Board, who, having

decided to relay the pitch a year before, failed to get the work underway until the autumn. The island's tourist board, though, had to deal with the consequences: 500 unhappy England supporters, who were offered a trip to the tourist resort of Ocho Rios. The country's government also tried to take the sting out of the situation by inviting them to a free drinks reception attended by both teams. There, Phil Tufnell happily revelled in the tactics he would have employed had he been called upon to bat. "I would have taken guard, left my bat standing in one of the cracks and run away," he said.

5

TOTAL **5**

Worst Bad Run

Marvan Atapattu, Sri Lanka v India, Australia, India again, New Zealand, Pakistan, West Indies, and India again, Chandigarh, Colombo, Ahmadebad, Dunedin, and Jamaica

November 1990 – November 1997.

It would be understating it to suggest Marvan Atapattu did not have a smooth introduction to international cricket. For Atapattu, who eventually established himself as Sanath Jayasuriya's opening partner for Sri Lanka, was forced to circumnavigate the globe for seven years in an ever-more-desperate search for a decent innings. His first six Test knocks were spectacularly tentative, and his return of just one run – off Greg Matthews, sandwiched between a pair of pairs against India – could have seen him forever consigned to that dark place in the outfield where the souls of the once promising wail, gnash and plead for just one more chance. As it was, three years did pass before he was deemed worthy of inclusion again, and two scores in the 20s against New Zealand in Dunedin won him a place in the side for Pakistan's visit; promoted to No 3 in Colombo, he responded with another duck. Opening in the second innings, he reached 25 before bailing out again, and his next two Tests brought him scores of just 14, 4, 7 and 10. Showing the kind of patience that might infer that Atapattu had possession of pictures of them in compromising positions, the selectors pressed on, and, on his eighth appearance, he rewarded them with a Test best 26, although when seen in the perspective of a match that produced four hundreds, one double and one triple century (as India replied with 537 for eight to Sri Lanka's 952 for six declared), it doesn't look that impressive. Finally, two more knocks of 29 against India put him in the mood for his return to Chandigarh, where his miserable journey had commenced, and he duly struck his first hundred, which set off a veritable catharsis of runs – five double centuries, five hundreds and a dozen or more fifties at the last count. One biographer has since observed, with great hindsight if not insight, that the Sri Lankan was a "vulnerable starter".

6

Worst Catch
Bruce Murray, Pakistan v New Zealand
3rd Test, Dacca, November 1969.

The worst catch ought really, by implication, to be a drop, but the usual rules have to be suspended when a scenario is enacted that is so absurd that even an ECB sub-committee would be hard pushed to dream it up after drinking the Long Room dry of Gordon's. Bruce Murray, a relatively minor figure in New Zealand cricket history, was the man singled out by fate to play the major role in the incident. Sent to field on the third-man boundary in Dacca, at this time still part of East Pakistan, Murray, a tall, loping figure from Wellington, was certainly not the first opposition cricketer to be greeted by having a

256

banana launched in his direction from the stands. He might, though, have been the only one to pick it up after it had rebounded off the back of his head and run with it towards gully, urging Dale Hadlee, in mid run-up, to stop. Others, including an umpire, joined Murray in his efforts, but by this time Hadlee was into his delivery stride and released the ball. Asif Iqbal flapped at the delivery, cutting it just backward of square, and Murray, still on the move, leapt full length to his right to take a spectacular one-handed catch, the banana still upright in his left hand. Despite New Zealand appeals, the umpires ruled the catch invalid on the basis of it being a dead ball. *The Auckland Star* banged the incident on its front page with barely disguised pun-ditry, branding it 'a peach of a catch'. Well, two can play at that game: let's just say it was an effort that was at once fruitful, yet fruitless.

7

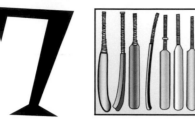

Worst Unfair Treatment
Ron Halcombe.
Victoria v Western Australia.
Melbourne. 1930.

What Ron Halcombe lacked in good fortune he made up for with innovation and application. Thus, instead of allowing himself to be dispirited by the loss of the top of his third finger on his right hand in an accident at the age of two, he took to doing special wrist exercises to compensate. Likewise, his lack of inches was counterbalanced by an ability to generate great pace; so much so that in the late 1920s, when the South Australian went west to Perth, he was considered the fastest bowler in the country and on the verge of

becoming the state's first Test representative. But all that was to change when, in a match against Victoria, he ran into umpire Andy Barlow. Barlow was also lacking in the digit department, First World War action in France in 1916 accounting for a thumb and ending his own playing ambitions. Whether that had hardened his outlook on Halcombe's own troubles is impossible to say, but he took the unusual step of going to watch the bowler in the nets the day before the match. Western Australia batted first, and were dismissed for under 200

258

before an enthusiastic Halcombe was thrown the ball to open the attack and, he hoped, advance his international prospects. But as he delivered his first ball, Halcombe was astonished to hear a no-ball call emanating from Barlow, at square leg; when he questioned it, he was told he was being called for throwing, and Barlow made the same judgment on the next four balls. By the time he had been no-balled eight times, Halcombe, who had played for two years without doubt being cast on his action, was reduced to bowling slow balls to complete the over. He did not bowl again in the match and was a ruined man when he returned to the dressing-room, regarding it as the end of his career. Although he was called several times in the subsequent match against Tasmania, he continued to play until the Second World War, being called only once again, while film of his action proved indecisive. Barlow, a Victorian, went on to umpire in 11 Tests, no-balling three other Australians for chucking and warning Keith Miller for intimidatory bowling. His integrity, according to one Australian cricket history, has never been questioned. Until now.

8

Worst Refereeing Controversy
Mike Denness. South Africa v India.
2nd Test. Port Elizabeth. November 2001.

As if dubious umpiring decisions were not enough, the ICC created another layer of potential controversy when it instituted the match referee system. Set up in reaction to perceived deteriorating standards of on-field behaviour, it was almost fated to result in a set of circumstances far outweighing the importance of the incident which produced them. When Mike Denness, the former England captain in charge of this game, saw television pictures of Sachin Tendulkar apparently lifting the seam on the fourth day, he swung into action with the same sense of duty he had shown when he dropped himself for the decisive Ashes Test of 1975, penalising him with a suspended one-match ban and a fine of 75 per cent of his match fee. But when he also came down hard on five further Indians for indiscretions ranging from dissent to intimidatory appealing, Jagmohan Dalmiya, the president of the Indian cricket board, was incensed, claiming that the Scotsman seemed to be abusing his powers by making such an example of one team. When the ICC refused to waver in its support for Denness, Dalmiya, with the assent of the South African board and the countries' respective governments, said they would not play the third Test in Pretoria if he was allowed, as scheduled, to referee that match too. When the ICC responded by withdrawing Test match status for the match, the teams went ahead and played an unofficial five-day international anyway. Denness may have over-reacted, but the Indian newspaper *The Hindu* saw colonialism at work, portraying him as "a no-nonsense headmaster from Eton whipping out his cane".

9

Worst Captaincy Moment
(part one)

Kim Hughes. Australia v West Indies.
2nd Test. Brisbane. November 1984.

Since Paul Gascoigne sobbed in the football World Cup semi-final against Germany, tears have became the ultimate fashion accessory to go with sporting achievement or disappointment. But six years before Gascoigne, the world was a different place, and Australians were poorly equipped to deal with the sight of the nation's captain breaking down in front of the cameras, and were left fidgeting with embarrassment as Kim Hughes, in between convulsive inhalations and exhalations, announced his resignation from the national captaincy. Hughes, who had become identified with the cricket establishment after taking over the reins from Graham Yallop in the wake of the Packer controversy, had grown weary of criticism from outside, but also internally from some fellow players who had since returned to the official Australian fray. As Bill Lawry poetically put it: "It was like being dragged down by a dingo in the pack and devoured by your own from without and within." Allan Border stepped into the breach with his country already 2-0 down, but if Hughes felt that his form would be helped without the pressures of captaincy, he was to get a swift reminder that the cricketing gods never let you off that easily: caught behind first ball off Joel Garner in the first innings of the third Test at Adelaide, he made two in the second innings, then lasted only three balls in recording a pair in the fourth at Melbourne. The selectors put him out of his misery by dropping him for the fifth at Sydney, where Australia got their only victory of the series by an innings and 55 runs.

10

Worst Captaincy Moment (part two)
Harry Trott. England v Australia
2nd Test. Old Trafford. July 1896.

Picture the scene: it is a hot summer's day on the first afternoon of a recent Ashes Test and, as usual, Steve Waugh and his partner are putting the English attack, also as usual cut to the bare bones by injury, to the sword. Suddenly, either through desperation or inspiration, Michael Vaughan makes a seemingly unprecedented move, ordering Alec Stewart to take off his pads and Mark Butcher to take over behind the stumps. Then he tells Stewart, whose ability with the ball is such that it is not even worthy of mention in the latest *Cricketers' Who's Who*, to measure out his run. Turning to deliver an assortment of off-breaks, leg-breaks and associated filth, he is as surprised as anyone when Waugh takes an outrageous swipe at a long hop, edges it, and watches aghast as it settles in Butcher's gloves. OK, so this scenario is an unlikely one, but scuttle back a little over a century and the plot seems familiar. WG Grace, captaining England, called upon Dick Lilley, with more than a hundred stumpings to his name, to bowl his only overs in Test cricket, after Harry Trott, the Australia skipper, had helped add 54 for the fourth wicket in 40 minutes. Trott obliged in the Waugh role, while John Thomas Brown, the opening batsman, played the Butcher part to perfection. The two main stars, though, went on to quite contrasting futures: Lilley was named Wisden Cricketer of the Year several months later, while Trott, obviously unable to live the incident down, went on to have a mental breakdown.

11

Worst Innings
Sunil Gavaskar. England v India
World Cup. Lord's. June 1975.

Truly bad innings are not the preserve of the tailender; by definition, such players are inept with a bat in their hands. No, the worst innings obviously must come from the blades of the best. Like Sunil Gavaskar, a man who had such difficulty in adapting to the requirements of one-day cricket that those who witnessed this particular performance were slowly sapped of the will to live. It was the inaugural World Cup, and England had made 334 for four from their 60 overs – a daunting total, it must be said, but one for which the masterful Indian opener might have been expected to have an answer. He could, for example, have laid the foundations for the middle

266

order to build on, and the tail to hammer into place, or he could have opted to try to bat through, keeping the score ticking over at one end while the strokemakers unleashed their sense of daring around him. Actually, the latter was the approach he adopted, though with a signficant variation. He was unbeaten at the end, but by striking one meagre boundary in a score of 36 from a monumental 174 balls, he had demoralised his team-mates to such an extent that they were able to muster only another 96 runs between them, India finishing on a totally inadequate 132 for three. It was not surprising that Gavaskar walked off to an accompaniment of boos from the crowd, but – worse – so indignant was one Indian supporter that he took his frustration out on a couple of policemen. Sentenced to a jail term of six months for assault, the time in prison must have passed in a flash compared to watching Gavaskar's effort.

Bibliography

Books

Chappell Greg: Unders and Overs: The Controversies of Cricket, *Lansdowne Press, 1981*

Plesse, Ken and Hansen, Brian: Wildmen of Cricket Volume One, *Hansen Publications, 1997*

Boon, David: Under the Southern Cross, The Autobiography, *Harper Sports, 1997*

Foot, David: Wally Hammond: The Reasons Why, *Robson Books, 1998*

McLean, Teresa: The Men in White Coats: Cricket Umpires Past and Present, *Stanley Paul, 1987*

Bose, Mihir: A History of Indian Cricket, *Andre Deutsch, 1990 and 2002*. Harte, Chris, A History of Australian Cricket, *Andre Deutsch, 1993*

Steen, Rob: Desmond Haynes: Lion of Barbados, *H F and G Witherby, 1993*

Martin-Jenkins, Christopher: World Cricketers: A Biographical Dictionary, *Oxford University Press, 1996*

Plesse, Ken: Cricket's Greatest Scandals, *Penguin Books Australia, 2000*
Robinson, Ray; The Wildest Tests, *Cassell, 1972 and 1979*

Fraser, David: The Man in White is Always Right: Cricket and the Law, *The Institute of Criminology, Sydney, 1993*

Reeve, Dermot (with Murphy, Pat): Winning Ways, *Boxtree, 1996*

Tibballs, Geoff: Great Sporting Mishaps, *Robson Books, 2001*

Winder, Robert: Hell for Leather: A Modern Cricket Journey, *Indigo 1996*

Waugh, Steve: Never Satisfied: A Diary of a Record-Breaking Year, *Harper Sports, 2000.*

Forsyth, Christopher: Pitched Battles: The History of Australia-England Test Cricket, *Visa, 1977*

Cashman, Richard and others (eds): The Oxford Companion to Australian Cricket, *Oxford University Press, 1996*

Cashman, Richard: 'Ave a Go, Yer Mug: Australian Cricket Crowds from Larrikin to Ocker, *Collins, 1984*

Richards, Viv (with Harris, Bob): Sir Vivian: The Definitive Autobiography, *Michael Joseph 2000*

Gatting, Mike (with Patmore, Amanda): Playing from the Front, *Futura, 1989*

Tufnell, Phil (with Hayter, Peter): What Now? The Autobiography, *HarperCollins Willow, 2000*

Botham, Ian: My Autobiography: Don't Tell Kath, *Collins Willow, 1994*

Nandy, Ashis: The Tao of Cricket: On Games of Destiny and the Destiny of Games, *Viking, 1989*

Brodribb, Gerald: Next Man In: A Survey of Cricket Laws and Customs, *Souvenir Press, 1995.*

Frindall, Bill (ed): The Wisden Book of Test Cricket Volume II: 1977-1994, *Headline, 1995*

Frindall, Bill (ed): The Wisden Book of Cricket Records, fourth edition, *Headline, 1998*

Jenner, Terry (with Piese, Ken): TJ: Over the Top, *Information Australia, 1999*

Wadhaney, K: Indian Cricket Controversies

Gillies, Angus: Adam Parore: The Wicked Keeper, *Penguin (NZ), 2002*

Newspapers

British: The Times, Today, The Guardian, The Daily Telegraph, The Daily Mail, South Wales Evening Post, Yorkshire Post

Australian: Sydney Morning Herald, Adelaide Advertiser, The Australasian, Hobart Mercury, The West Australian, The Age.

Caribbean: The Daily Gleaner (Jamaica); The Nation (Barbados), The Trinidad Guardian.

New Zealand: Auckland Star Indian: The Hindu

Magazines

The Cricketer, Wisden Cricket Monthly,
Third Man, Inside Edge

Websites

Cricinfo.com